COLORADO
PLACE ✦ NAMES

COLORADO
PLACE ✦ NAMES

W I L L I A M   B R I G H T

Johnson Books: Boulder

Library of Congress Cataloging-in-Publication Data
  Bright, William, 1928–
    Colorado Place Names / William Bright.
      p.   cm.
    Includes bibliographical references (p.).
    ISBN 1-55566-102-5 (paper)
      1. Names, Geographical—Colorado.   2. Colorado—History, Local.
  I. Title.
  F774.B75   1993
  917.88'003—dc20   93-777
                                                                          CIP

Cover Design: Bob Schram/Bookends
Cover Photograph: Mount Princeton by Eric J. Wunrow

1   2   3   4   5   6   7   8   9

Printed in the United States of America by
Johnson Printing Company
1880 South 57th Court
Boulder, Colorado 80301

CONTENTS

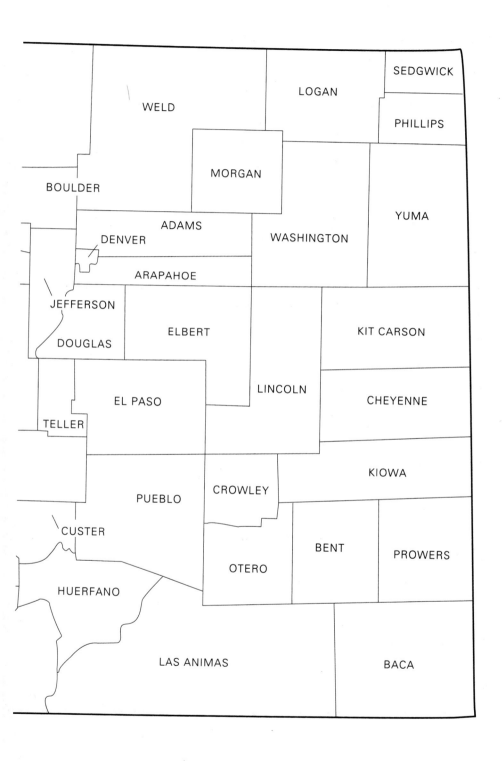

INTRODUCTION

This book is a direct descendant of the excellent *Colorado Place Names,* by George R. Eichler (Boulder: Johnson Publishers, 1977). Most of the information in the present volume, and much of the actual wording, is drawn from Eichler's work. If he had lived to prepare a revised edition— or a much larger reference work on Colorado places, as he hoped—my effort would not have been warranted.

The question arises of exactly what should be included in a dictionary of place names. Such a work is not the same as a gazetteer, which provides detailed geographical and historical information for each place listed. A place name dictionary seeks to give information not so much on the *places* as on the *names*: how they are pronounced, how they came to be, when they were assigned. Geographical information, such as location, population, historical facts, and the dates when communities were established and incorporated, are given for orientation and for background. I have not given all the historical information provided by Eichler; I wanted to include other types of information, and the book had to be kept within practical limits.

In fact, I have gone beyond a simple revision of my predecessor's book. Eichler listed towns, counties, peaks, and passes in separate sections; I have combined these in a single alphabetical order, and have added entries for rivers, creeks, lakes, valleys, parks, and other topographic features. In particular, I have given more information on pronunciation; and reflecting my own research in linguistics, I have given special attention to names of Spanish and American Indian origin.

To be sure, the list is still far from complete. There are eighteen streams in Colorado called Coal Creek; I have mentioned them as a group, and singled out only the one which gave its name to a town in Fremont County. Many communities formed in recent years have names invented by real estate developers, such as Mountain View or Sunnyside, concerning which little can be said. (Eichler appropriately referred to these as "generic names.") Apart from that, information is simply lacking about many places: given that a ghost town exists with the name of Johnsonville, it may not be possible to find out much about it except that it was named after a "Mr. Johnson." In the end, out of an excessively long list of place names that might be included here, I have given preference to those of major population centers, of recreational sites frequently visited, and of significant places in the history of Colorado—as well as to names whose origins are less obvious, especially those of American Indian origin.

Much information about Colorado place names remains uncertain or undiscovered. I am most grateful to all the people inside and outside Colorado who have provided me with rare facts; they are listed under "Acknowledgments." I am especially indebted to members of the Language and Culture Commitee of the Southern Ute Indian Tribe, in Ignacio, for help with Native American place names. I will be equally grateful to all those people who can provide me with further corrections and clarifications.

W. B.

PRONUNCIATION

The pronunciation of many Colorado place names is obvious from their spelling. In other cases, however, this book indicates pronunciations phonetically within brackets. The phonetic symbols used are those of the *Random House Dictionary of the English Language,* but similar systems are used in other familiar English dictionaries. The values of symbols are as follows:

[a]   as in *cap, bad, act.*
[ā]   *cape, save, day.*
[â]   *care, fair, carrot.*
[ä]   *far, father, spa.*
[ch]   *child, church.*
[e]   *set, red, left.*
[ē]   *eve, east, seed.*
[ə]   the unaccented *a* of *sofa, appear, alone.*
[g]   *go, give, gag.*
[i]   *it, bid, ink.*
[ī]   *ice, side, fine.*
[ng]   *sing, long.*
[o]   *cot, fond, collie.* Most Americans pronounce this the same as the [ä] in *father.*
[ō]   *oak, over, own.*
[ô]   *law, dawn, caught.* Many Coloradans pronounce this the same as the [o] in *cot* and the [ä] in *father.*
[oi]   *boil, boy, coin.*
[o͝o]   *book, look, put.*
[o͞o]   *boot, soon, coop.*
[ou]   *out, loud, down.*
[th]   *thin, thick, think.*
[u]   *up, sun, love.*
[û]   *urge, bird, term.*

The syllable with principal accent has a "prime" mark after it; that is, a name like Como, [kō´ mō], is pronounced "KO-mo."

Many Colorado place names, especially those of Spanish origin, have more than one current pronunciation. Rather than label one pronunciation as more "correct" than another, it is preferable to note that different pronunciations tend to be used by people of different backgrounds. Thus "Colorado" is orginally a Spanish word, pronounced approximately [kō lō rä′ dō], but several English adaptations of this have been made. An old-fashioned pronunciation among Anglos is [kol ə rā′ dō], but this is now seldom heard; most native Coloradans say [kol ə rad′ ō], although recent immigrants to the state may say [kol ə rä′ dō]. Nowadays, since many Coloradans have been exposed to Spanish in school, there is a tendency to restore pronunciations closer to the original Spanish; thus, although "Mosca" has a traditional Anglo pronunciation [mos′ kə], it is now sometimes pronounced [mō′ skə], with the Spanish vowel quality in the first syllable.

ABBREVIATIONS

Co. County
Est. Established
Inc. Incorporated
Pop. Population (1990 Census)

Abarr [ab′ är], in the sand hills of Yuma County (est. 1921), was founded by Dr. D. C. Brown, with the name of Brownsville. In 1923, S. E. Hoffman started a store and had the town site surveyed, platted, and recorded. When a post office was opened, because there was another Colorado town named Brownsville, the name was changed to Abarr, the maiden name of Hoffman's wife.

Abeyta [ə bā′ tə], in Las Animas County, is a Spanish family name.

Acequia [ä sē kwē′ ə], a locale in Douglas County, takes its name from the Spanish word for "irrigation ditch." A pronunciation closer to Spanish would be [ä sä′ kē ä].

Achonee [ə chō′ nē], **Mount,** in Indian Peaks Wilderness, Grand County (12,649 ft.). Probably named for a Cheyenne sub-chief, Ochanee or Ochinee, meaning "one-eye," who was killed at the Sand Creek Massacre in 1864.

Acoma [ak′ ō mə], **Mount,** in Rocky Mountain National Park, Grand County (10,508 ft.). Named for the Acoma Indian tribe in New Mexico; the name means "white rock people" in their language. The same name, as applied to a street in Denver, is often pronounced [ə kō′ mə].

Adams City, on U.S. 85 in Adams County (est. 1923), was named for the county. **Adams County** (est. 1902, area 1,237 sq. mi., pop. 265,038), which has Brighton as its seat, was named for Alva Adams, who served two terms as governor in 1887 to 1889 and 1897 to 1899, plus sixty days in 1905. Separately named are **Adams Lake** and **Mount Adams** (12,121 ft.), in Rocky Mountain National Park, Grand County. Named perhaps for J. E. Adams, or perhaps for Alexander Adams, a resident of Grand Lake.

Adena [ə dē′ nə], a locale in Morgan County, was named for Edna Adena, sweetheart of an early settler.

Adobe [ə dō´ bē] **Creek** is the name of four streams in Colorado. The Spanish word *adobe* designates a claylike soil from which it is possible to make sun-baked bricks; or it can refer to a house constructed of such bricks.

Aetna [et´ nə], **Mount,** in Chaffee County (13,771 ft.). Named after Mount Aetna or Etna, a volcano in Sicily.

Agate [ag´ ət], on U.S. 40 and 287 in Elbert County (est. 1876?). While the origin of the name is unverified, it is believed the Union Pacific Railroad selected the name. One authority states the name reflects agate (rock) specimens found in the area, and Indian arrowheads made of the same variety of chalcedony quartz. Another story is that there was a large gate on the townsite through which travelers passed. Gradually the words were fused in pronunciation and written as one: A Gate to Agate. An earlier name was Gebhard.

Agua, Spanish for "water," occurs in many place names; in Colorado English, it is usually pronounced [ä´ wə]. **Agua Fria** [frē´ ə] **Lake,** in Jackson County, is Spanish for "cold water." **Agua Ramon** [rə mōn´], also written Aqua Ramon, is a locale in Rio Grande County; Spanish *Agua Ramón* means "the water (or spring) of Raymond."

Aguascosa [ä wä skō´ sə] **Lake** (also written Acascosa), in Conejos County, probably represents Spanish *agua ascosa* "stagnant water."

Aguazul [ä wä sōōl´], a stream in Saguache County, is from Spanish *agua azul* "blue water."

Aguilar [ag´ i lär], town on the Apishapa River in Las Animas County (est. 1867, inc. 1894; pop. 520). A more old-fashioned pronunciation is [ag´ wi lär]. First a trading post for Indians and Spanish-American farmers, the town was founded by Agapita Rivali. When the town sought incorporation it was named for José Ramón Aguilar, a prominent pioneer of southern Colorado. The Spanish surname literally means "eagle's nest," from *águila* "eagle."

Ajax [ā´ jaks] **Peak,** in San Miguel County (12,785 ft.), named for a Greek hero of the Trojan War.

Akron [ak´ rən], town on U.S. 34, seat of Washington County (est. 1882, inc. 1887, pop. 1,599). Named by a Mrs. Calvert, wife of a railroad official, for her home town, Akron, Ohio. The name is Greek, meaning "summit," and was considered appropriate because the town was supposedly on the highest point of the Chicago, Burlington & Quincy Railroad in Colorado.

Alamaditas [al′ ə mə dē′ təs] **Mesa,** in Conejos County, is perhaps for Spanish *alameditas* "little groves," diminutive plural of *alameda* "grove of trees."

Alameda [al ə mē′ də], in Jefferson County, is Spanish for "a cottonwood grove," or more generally a grove or avenue of ornamental trees.

Alamo [al′ ə mō], in Huerfano County, represents Spanish *álamo* "cottonwood tree."

Alamosa [al ə mō′ sə], city on the Rio Grande River and on Highway 285 (est. and inc. 1878, pop. 7,579). More old-fashioned pronunciations are [al ə mo͞o′ sē] or [al ə mo͞o′ sə]. Founded by Governor Alexander C. Hunt, president of the Denver and Rio Grande Construction Company. He gave it the name of nearby **Alamosa Creek,** which had been named by early Spanish settlers, using a Spanish feminine adjective meaning "full of cottonwoods." This word is in turn from Spanish *álamo* "cottonwood tree," a common place name throughout the American southwest. An earlier settlement on the site was Wayside, a stagecoach stop (est. 1876); this was abandoned before the platting of the present town. The modern city is the seat of **Alamosa County** (est. 1913, area 719 sq. mi., pop. 13,617). This is the most recently created county in the state, having been formed from portions of Costilla and Conejos counties; it was named after the city. **East Alamosa** (pop. 1,389) is a nearby community.

Alamosita [al ə mō sē′ tə] **Creek,** in Costilla County. The Spanish term means "little cottonwood grove," being the diminutive of *alamosa.*

Albion [al′ bē ən], **Mount,** a peak in Boulder County (12,609 ft.). The name Albion is a poetic term for Great Britain. Until 1915 this mountain was called Sheep Mountain, while the name Mount Albion was applied to a nearby mountain which is now called Kiowa Peak.

Alder, the tree *Alnus tenuifolia,* gives its name to five streams named **Alder Creek** in Colorado. One of these has in turn given its name to **Alder,** a locale on U.S. 285 in Saguache County.

Alexander Mountain, in Larimer County (7,105 ft.), is named for the pioneers John and Grant Alexander.

Alice, in Clear Creek County, was named by a miner named Taylor for his wife Alice. **Mount Alice,** in Rocky Mountain National Park, Boulder and Grand counties (13,310 ft.), has a name dating from 1905, but the origin is not known.

Alkali [al′ kə lī] is a term referring to soluble minerals often found in springs or streams, generally making them unsuitable for drinking or agriculture. The term occurs in many Colorado place names; thus there are seven streams called **Alkali Creek.**

Allens Park, also written as Allenspark, community on Colorado 7 in Boulder County. Named for an early settler, Alonzo Allen, who homesteaded in 1864. The first post office, built in the 1870s, was destroyed by fire in 1894. A later one was built two miles from the original site, and the site was platted in 1897.

Allison, on Colorado 151 in La Plata County, on the Southern Ute Indian Reservation (est. 1901). First called Vallejo, it was changed by postal authorities because of confusion with a California town. The new name was selected by the residents to honor Allison Stocker, a pioneer contractor and builder of many Denver buildings, and prominent in the development of this area of La Plata County.

Alma [al′ mə], town on Colorado 9 in Park County (est. 1872, inc. 1873, pop. 148). Three explanations for the name exist: that it was named for Alma James, wife of a Fairplay merchant who opened the first store there; that it was named for Alma Graves, wife of Abner Graves, who operated the Alma Mine; and that it was named for Alma Jaynes, popular daughter of an early settler.

Almagre [äl mä′ grā] **Mountain,** in Teller County (12,367 ft.). The Spanish word means "red ochre," a type of earth containing reddish iron oxide.

Almont [al′ mont], on Colorado 135 in Gunnison County (est. 1881). Sam Fisher, an early and prominent Gunnison County rancher, purchased a fine stallion, son of the famous Almont of Kentucky. When the Denver and Rio Grande Railroad was built to Fisher's ranch and a town grew up there in 1881, the settlement was named for the great race horse that had sired Fisher's stallion.

Alpine, in Rio Grande County, named for the Alps of Europe. There is also an **Alpine** in Chaffee County, formerly the railhead for the Denver,

South Park and Pacific Railroad, which from 1882 to 1910 ran through the **Alpine Tunnel** (on the Continental Divide, Chaffee, and Gunnison counties, 11,524 ft.) to Gunnison.

Altura [al tōō´ rə], the name of places in Archuleta, Arapahoe, and Adams counties, is Spanish for "high place," derived from *alto* "high."

Alverjones [äl vûr hō´ näs] **Lake,** in Conejos County. In the Spanish of New Mexico and Colorado, the term refers to a type of peas.

Amherst [am´ ərst], on Colorado 176 in Phillips County (est. 1887?). Supposedly named by an early rancher from Amherst, Massachusetts, who settled in Colorado. Many communities were named by early residents for their former "back east" towns, sometimes inspired by homesickness.

Americus [ə mâr´ i kəs], in Chaffee County, is the Latin form for the name of Amerigo Vespucci (1451–1512), the Italian merchant after whom America was named.

Amity [am´ i tē], in Prowers County, was founded by members of the Salvation Army in 1898, after problems over the building of Amity Canal had been solved.

Anaconda [an ə kon´ də], in Teller County. Probably named for the famous Anaconda copper mine in Montana, which was named in turn (for its size) after a huge South American snake.

Anasazi [an ə sä´ zē] **Heritage Center,** in Montezuma County, is a museum of the prehistoric culture of the Four Corners region. The term Anasazi refers to pueblo dwellers who flourished from around A.D. 100 to 1300. The name is borrowed from Navajo *anaasázi* "enemies' ancestors," the term "enemies" being used by the Navajo to designate the modern Pueblo tribes of the southwest.

Andrews Peak, in Rocky Mountain National Park, Grand and Larimer counties (12,565 ft.). Officially named in 1932, perhaps after Darwin M. Andrews, a Boulder botanizer and photographer. There is an **Andrews Lake** in San Juan County.

Animas [an´ i məs] **River,** in La Plata County, originally had the Spanish name *Río de Las Ánimas Perdidas* "River of the Lost Souls." **Animas Forks** was founded as a mining settlement near the river's headwaters. **Animas Mountain** is nearby in San Juan County (13,786 ft.). These names are not to be confused with the *Río de las Ánimas Perdidas en Purgatorio* "River of the Lost Souls in Purgatory" in southeastern Colorado (now called the Purgatoire River), which gave its name to Las Animas County and to the town of Las Animas.

Antelope is a name commonly given in the western United States to the animal also called the "pronghorn," *Antilocapra americana*; it is not related to the African antelope. Fourteen streams in Colorado are called **Antelope Creek.**

Antero [an târ′ ō] **Junction,** at the joining of U.S. 24 and 285 in Park County (est. 1892?), was named for the Uintah Ute Chief Antero—one of the chiefs who, in 1873, signed a treaty ceding rich mineral lands in the San Juan district to the United States. The same name is borne by the nearby **Antero Reservoir,** as well as **Mount Antero,** a peak some distance away in Chaffee County (14,269 ft.).

Anthracite [an′ thrə sīt] **Pass,** in Gunnison County (10,150 ft.), is named for a hard variety of coal.

Antlers, on U.S. 6 in Garfield County, is said to have been named by Henry A. Butters, the founder of the town, for the Antlers Hotel in Colorado Springs.

Anton [an′ ton], on U.S. 36 in Washington County (est. 1920?). It is claimed that the homesteader Maurice S. Walters turned in the name Canton—after the town of Canton, Nebraska—when suggestions were asked for naming a new post office and store. His suggestion was misread as Anton.

Antonito [an tə nē′ tō], town on U.S. 285 in Conejos County (est. 1881, inc. 1889, pop. 875); also pronounced [an tə nē′ tə]. Founded by the Denver and Rio Grande Railroad; the Spanish name is the diminutive of *Antonio* "Anthony," after the San Antonio Mountains and San Antonio River in the vicinity.

Antora [an tōr′ ə] **Peak,** in Saguache County (13,266 ft.), apparently of Ute origin. Perhaps a variant of the name Antero (see above).

Apache [ə pach′ ē] **City,** on U.S. 85 and 87 in Huerfano County, was named for an American Indian group of the Southwest. The name was formerly also applied to the Navajo, and is derived from Zuni *apachu* "Navajo." There are also four streams named **Apache Creek** in Colorado.

Apache Peak is in Rocky Mountain National Park, in Grand and Boulder counties (13,441 ft.); its name was proposed in 1914, as one of several in the Indian Peaks area.

Apex [ā′ peks], on Pine Creek in Gilpin County; from the Latin for "peak."

Apiatan Mountain, in Grand County (10,319 ft.), was named for a Kiowa chief, a singer of songs which were published in Natalie Curtis's *The Indian Book* (1910). His name is said to refer to a wooden ceremonial lance.

Apishapa [ə pish′ ə pə] **River,** is a tributary of the Arkansas River; it flows through Las Animas, Pueblo, and Otero counties. Said to be from the Ute for "standing or stagnant water." At one time folk-etymologized into "Fish-Paw River."

Arapahoe [ə rap′ ə hō], on U.S. 40 in Cheyenne County (est. 1870). Named for the principal Indian tribe of the region; the name is also spelled "Arapaho." This is not the name that the Arapaho people use for themselves; it is said to be derived from Pawnee *tiraapuhu'* "he is bartering" or *iriiraraapuhu* "trader." However, the Pawnee do not use this term to refer to the Arapaho, so it may have been misunderstood by whites. Another possible source is Crow *aa-raxpé-ahu,* literally "tattoo." **Arapahoe County** (est. 1861, area 797 sq. mi., pop. 391,511) was named independently; the county seat is Littleton. This was the first designated county in Colorado Territory. **Arapaho Pass** is between Grand and Boulder counties (11,906 ft.). Nearby are **North Arapaho Peak** (13,502 ft.), and **South Arapaho Peak** (13,397 ft.); these mountains, forming part of the Indian Peaks group, were named around 1877.

Arboles [är′ bō lēz], on Colorado 151 in Archuleta County, on the Southern Ute Indian Reservation (est. 1881); also pronounced [är′ bō ləs]. From Spanish *árboles* "trees," referring to the wooded growth along the banks of the nearby Piedra River.

Archuleta [är chōō let′ ə] **County** (est. 1885, area 1,364 sq. mi., pop. 5,345). The county seat is Pagosa Springs. In honor of Antonio D. Archuleta, who was a senator from Conejos County when it was divided to form Archuleta County.

Arena [ə rē′ nə], in Cheyenne County, is the Spanish word for "sand."

Argentine Pass, between Summit and Clear Creek counties (13,132 ft.), and **Argentine Peak,** in Clear Creek County (13,738 ft.), were both probably named not for the South American nation of Argentina, but rather with a term derived from Latin *argentum* "silver."

Arickaree [ə rik′ ə rē], on U.S. 36 in Washington County, was named for an Indian tribe of the Dakotas, also termed Arikaree, Arikara, or Ree. A Spanish recording of 1794 lists *Alicara* as the name of one band within the tribe. It has been claimed that the name comes from Pawnee *paariiku'* "horn" or *arikaraaru'* "buck deer," referring to a custom of wearing two pieces of bone in the hair, standing up like horns; however, this is not in fact the Pawnee name for the Arikara. **Arikaree Peak,** in Grand and Boulder counties (13,150 ft.), was officially named in 1914 as one of the Indian Peaks group. There is also an **Arikaree River** in Yuma County.

Arkansas [är′ kən sô] **River,** flows through Lake, Chaffee, Fremont, Pueblo, Otero, Bent, and Prowers counties, eastward through the states of Kansas, Oklahoma, and Arkansas, where it joins the Mississippi. Originally the plural of *Arkansa,* a tribal name which entered French as early as 1673. The term was originally *aakansa,* an Algonkian name for a Siouan Indian group. In the state of Kansas, the river is sometimes given the alternative pronunciation [är kan′ zəs], by analogy with the name of the state.

Arlington, on Colorado 96 in Kiowa county (est. 1887). Founded as Juliet, its present name was given by the Missouri Pacific Railroad, and honors one of its officials.

Armel [är mel′], in Yuma County, was named for a storekeeper, Armel Bremmgro.

Aroya [ə roy′ ə], on Colorado 94 in Cheyenne County (est. 1872), is a corruption of Spanish *arroyo* "creek." The town is built on the site of the ranch owned by T. C. Schilling, one of the founders of the Schilling Tea Co.

Arrastre [ə ras′ trə] **Creek,** the name of streams in Alamosa and San Juan counties (also spelled "Arrastra"), from Spanish *arrastre,* a crude stone device used by miners to crush quartz.

Arriba [âr′ i bə], town on U.S. 24 in Lincoln County (est. 1898, inc. 1918, pop. 220). A Spanish word meaning "above," referring to the town's altitude (5,239 ft.) compared with others in the region. As the name of a town in New Mexico, this is pronounced [ə rē′ bə], which is closer to the original Spanish pronunciation.

Arriola [ä rē ō´ lə], on U.S. 666 in Montezuma County (est. 1885?); also pronounced [âr ē ō´ lə]. Named for an early Spanish military man, but no details are recorded.

Arroyo [ə roi´ ō], a Spanish word for "creek," occurs in many Colorado place names. Thus **Arroyo Escondido,** a stream in Archuleta County, means "hidden creek." **Arroyo Hondo,** in Huerfano County, means "deep creek."

Artesia [är tē´ zhə], in Moffat County, is the Latin name for Artois, a town in France for which "artesian" wells are named. The name was given because of the water supply for the Rangely oil field development.

Arvada [är vad´ ə], city on Colorado 121 in Adams and Jefferson counties (est. 1880, inc. 1904, pop. 89,235). Named for Hiram Arvada Hoskin, brother-in-law of the wife of the founder, Benjamin Franklin Wadsworth (whose name is still borne by the main thoroughfare). In 1860 it was known as Ralston Point and Ralston Station, for the creek where early placer miners first discovered "color" in their gold pans.

Aspen, city on the Roaring Fork River and on Colorado 82 (est. 1880, inc. 1881, pop. 5,049); the seat of Pitkin County. It was previously called Ute City; but the townsite surveyor, B. Clark Wheeler, named the town for the profuse growth of quaking aspen trees (*Populus tremuloides*) in the vicinity.

Association Camp, near Estes Park in Larimer County, was named in 1911 because of the camp founded by the YMCA (Young Men's Christian Association).

Atchee [ach´ ē], in Garfield County, was named for a local Ute chief, an advocate of peaceful relations.

Atwood, on U.S. 6 in Logan County (est. 1885), was named by Victor Wilson, who brought a colony from Abilene, Kansas. Wilson, a Unitarian, named the town for a minister of his church, the Reverend John S. Atwood of Boston, Massachusetts.

Audubon [ô´ də bon], **Mount,** in Boulder County (12,223 ft.), was named for the painter and naturalist John James Audubon (1780–1851).

Ault [ôlt], town on U.S. 85 in Weld County (est. 1888, inc. 1904, pop. 1,107), was named for Alexander Ault, pioneer miller of Fort Collins. Ault purchased the entire crop raised in the area for many years before grain storage facilities were available in the vicinity. For this service to the community the town adopted his name when a post office was established in 1904.

Auraria [ōr âr′ ē ə], a mining camp adjacent to Denver, founded in 1858, later absorbed into Denver. Named by one of its founders for his home town, Auraria, Georgia; the term is Latin for "gold mine," from *aurum* "gold."

Aurora [ə rōr′ ə], city on U.S. 40 and 287 in Adams and Arapahoe counties (est. 1891, inc. 1903, pop. 222,103). First named Fletcher, for Donald Fletcher, one of the town promoters. The name was changed to its present one upon incorporation because town officials thought the new name "classier." The name is a Latin word meaning "dawn" or "morning."

Austin, on Colorado 922 in Delta County (est. 1900, post office est. 1905). Named for Austin Miller, rancher and land-owner, who gave the Denver and Rio Grande Railroad land for its right of way and the townsite.

Avalanche [av′ ə lanch] **Peak,** in Eagle County (12,803 ft.), refers to the possibility of disastrous snow slides.

Avalo [av′ ə lō], in Weld County, is perhaps from a Spanish word for "earthquake"; however, it may also be from a Spanish family name *Avalos*.

Avon [ē′ vən], town on the Eagle River and on U.S. 6, in Eagle County (est. 1884, pop. 1,798). Thought to have been named by an Englishman for England's Avon River. When it was listed as a railroad station in 1889, it was spelled Avin, and later changed to its present spelling.

Avondale [ē′ vən dēl], on U.S. 50 in Pueblo County (est. 1890?). An Englishman, Sam Taylor, one of the pioneer settlers, named it for his old home, Stratford-on-Avon, England. Earlier it was known as Forest Park.

Axial [ak′ sē əl], in Moffatt County, is said to have been so named by Major John Wesley Powell because the valley in which it lies formed the axis of the geological upheaval which raised the surrounding mountains, creating the surrounding coal and mineral area.

Baca [bak´ ə] **County** (est. 1889, area 2,563 sq. mi., pop. 4,556) was named for the Baca family of Trinidad, a member of which was the first settler on Two Buttes Creek. The county was created from the eastern portion of Las Animas County; its seat is Springfield.

Bachicha [bə chē´ chə] **Creek** in Las Animas County; the name is also written as Bachichi, Vachita, Vachicha, and Vachiche. Derived from a Spanish surname.

Badito [bə dī´ tō], on the Huerfano River and Colorado 69, in Huerfano County. Probably from Spanish *vadito* "little ford," diminutive of *vado* "ford."

Bailey, on U.S. 285 in Park County (est. 1864). Named for a settler, William Bailey, who established a hotel and stage station in 1864. Known as Bailey's Ranch, the station's name was shortened and used by the settlement. In 1878, the narrow-gauge Denver, South Park and Pacific Railroad made Bailey its terminal.

Baker Mountain, in Rocky Mountain National Park, on the Continental Divide between Jackson and Grand counties (12,397 ft.). Named for John R. Baker, who first climbed the peak in 1875.

Bald Mountain is the name of fifteen peaks in Colorado; the highest is in Summit County (13,679 ft.). But **Baldy Mountain,** in San Juan County, is said to have been named for Brigadier General George Baldy.

Balzac [bôl´ zak], in Morgan County, was probably named after the French novelist Honoré de Balzac (1799–1850). There is also a **Balzac Gulch** in Garfield County.

Barela [bä rel´ ə], on San Francisco Creek in Las Animas County, was named for Senator Casimiro Barela, who served in the territorial legislature.

Barnesville, in Weld County (est. 1908), bears the family name of Charles and George Barnes.

Barr Lake, a locale on U.S. 6 in Adams County, was named for an adjacent reservoir, named in turn for a civil engineer of the Chicago, Burlington, and Quincy Railroad.

Bartlett, on U.S. 160 in Baca County (est. 1928). When the Santa Fe Railway built a branch line through here to the town of Pritchett, the section point was named for an official of the railroad.

Barton, in Prowers County, was the surname of an XY Ranch clerk around 1905.

Basalt [bə sôlt′], town on Colorado 82 in Eagle and Pitkin counties (est. 1882, inc. 1901, pop. 1,128), was named for nearby **Basalt Peak** (10,800 ft.). The name refers to a dark, dense, igneous rock produced in lava flows.

Battle Mountain is the name of three peaks in the state. The highest, in Rocky Mountain National Park, Larimer County (12,044 ft.), was named by Enos Mills, referring to the visible effects of wind, snow, and fire.

Baxter, on U.S. business route 50 in Pueblo County (est. 1859?), was named for Oliver H. P. Baxter, the owner of the land on which the settlement was founded. But **Baxter Pass,** in Garfield County (8,422 ft.) was named for C. O. Baxter, the engineer who built the railway on this route. There is a **Baxter Mountain** in Saguache County (11,727 ft.), and a **Baxter Peak** in Garfield County (11,185 ft.). Independently named is **Baxterville,** on Colorado 49 in Rio Grande County; this name is said to honor a Mr. Baxter, the owner of a small restaurant there, who was famous for his chili.

Bayfield, town on the Los Pinos River and U.S. 160, in La Plata County (est. 1886, inc. 1906, pop. 1,090). Named for W. A. Bay, who laid out the town plan. The post office was formerly Los Pinos.

Bear, referring either to the grizzly bear (*Ursus horribilis,* now probably extinct in Colorado) or to the black bear (*Ursus americanus,* which may be "cinnamon" as well as black), is a term used widely in Colorado place names. **Bear River** is a locality on the Yampa River and U.S. 40 in Routt County. There are also thirty streams called **Bear Creek,** as well as sixteen called **Bear Gulch** and eleven places called **Bear Canyon.** Eight bodies of water are called **Bear Lake.** Eleven summits are called **Bear Mountain;** the highest is in San Juan County (12,987 ft.). The name **Bear Peak** is also given to two mountains. **Bear Valley** is a postal station in Denver.

Beaver, a familiar amphibious rodent (*Castor canadensis*), gives its name to twenty-seven streams in Colorado called **Beaver Creek;** the one near

Vail, in Eagle County, has become well known as the site of a ski resort. A **Beaver Lake** is nearby, but there are nine others so named in the state. Four peaks are called **Beaver Mountain,** the highest of which is in Rio Grande County (11,528 ft.). **Beaver Point** is a locale on U.S. 36 in Larimer County.

Beckwith Mountain, East (12,432 ft.), and **West Beckwith Mountain** (12,185 ft.), are in Gunnison County. They are named for Lieutenant E. G. Beckwith, second in command to Captain John Gunnison on his expedition of 1853 to explore a railroad route through Colorado.

Bedrock, on Colorado 90 in Montrose County (est. 1883), was probably so named because the general store and post office was built in 1883 on a bedrock of sandstone.

Beecher Island, a locality on the Arikaree River in Yuma County, was named for Lieutenant Fred Beecher, who was killed there in a battle with Indians in 1868.

Belford [bel′ fərd], **Mount,** in Chaffee County (14,197 ft.), was named for Territorial Judge James B. Belford, appointed by President Ulysses S. Grant in 1870. He retired from the bench in 1875; and when Colorado became a state in 1876, he was elected as the first Colorado member of the U.S. House of Representatives. In Washington he was nicknamed the "Red-Headed Rooster of the Rockies" because of his colorful manner and appearance. The mountain named for him was a latecomer to the roster of the 14,000-foot peaks, as it was previously considered part of Mount Oxford. Later surveys added height, designating it as a separate peak.

Belle Plain, in Pueblo County, is intended to be French for "beautiful plain."

Bellvue [bel′ vyo͞o], in Larimer County (est. 1882), is from French *belle vue* "beautiful view." It was so named by founder Jacob Fowler in 1882; he was one of the first to show that fruit could successfully be grown in Colorado. The spelling was distorted by the postal authorities to Bellvue. There is also a **Belleview** on Colorado 291 in Chaffee County.

Belmar, a postal station in Jefferson County. The word is a common Spanish surname.

Belmont, a postal station in Pueblo. From French *bel mont* "beautiful mountain."

Bennett, town on Colorado 36 and 79 in Adams County (est. 1870, inc. 1930, pop. 1,757), named for H. P. Bennett, an early postmaster of Denver. First called Kiowa, for nearby Kiowa Creek; the term refers to an Indian tribe of the southern plains.

Bent County (est. 1874, area 1,519 sq. mi., pop. 5,048). The county seat is Las Animas. From the famous Bent's Fort, founded by the brothers Charles and William Bent and Ceran St. Vrain from St. Louis; in 1833 they established a trading post and Santa Fe Trail depot on the north bank of the Arkansas River, midway between La Junta and Las Animas. The county was created from a portion of Greenwood County, which was established in 1870 and abolished in 1874. **Bent's Old Fort,** a national historic site, is now in Otero County.

Bergen Park, on Colorado 74 in Jefferson County (est. 1859), was named for Thomas C. Bergen, one of the earliest settlers west of Denver. He managed a hotel and stage station, and the area assumed his name.

Berthoud [bûr′ thəd], town on U.S. 287 in Larimer County (est. 1877, inc. 1888, pop. 2,990), was named for Captain Edward L. Berthoud, chief civil engineer of the Colorado Central Railroad when the line reached here. The settlement earlier was known as Little Thompson, after the river of that name; a post office opened in the spring of 1875. Also named for the captain is the route he discovered over **Berthoud Pass,** on the Continental Divide, between Clear Creek and Grand counties (11,315 ft.).

Berts Corner, on U.S. 287 in Larimer County (est. 1935?), was named for Bert Foote, who operated a filling station and had tourist cabins there in the 1930s.

Beshoar [besh′ ōr] **Junction,** at the meeting of U.S. 160 and 350, in Las Animas County (est. 1888?), was named for Michael Beshoar, pioneer physician, an early and colorful settler of Trinidad.

Bethune [beth o͞on′], town on U.S. 24 in Kit Carson County (est. 1918, inc. 1926, pop. 173). Founded during World War I, it was named for a town in France.

Beulah [byo͞o′ lə], in Pueblo County (est. 1862), was first known as Mace's Hole, because a Mexican outlaw, Juan Mace, once made the valley his hiding place. Later, a Reverend Gaylord settled there and, feeling that the name Mace's Hole lacked beauty, suggested the present name.

When a vote was taken at a social gathering, the name Beulah, Hebrew for "married" or "inhabited," won by two votes over the name Silver Glen. Although the name Beulah refers in the Bible to the vague but blessed land of the future (Isaiah 62:4), its popular usage is based more directly upon its occurrence in John Bunyan's *Pilgrim's Progress.*

Bierstadt [bēr′ städ], **Mount,** in Clear Creek County (14,060 ft.), was named for Albert Bierstadt (1830–1902), an artist whose paintings of the Rockies became world famous; three were painted for the Capitol in Washington, D.C. One of his most popular is "Storm over the Rockies," with Mount Evans as the model. **Bierstadt Lake,** in Rocky Mountain National Park, Larimer County, is also named for the painter, who visited the area in 1876 and 1877.

Bighorn Mountain, in Rocky Mountain National Park, Larimer County (11,463 ft.), is named for the bighorn sheep (*Ovis canadensis*), also called the mountain sheep or Rocky Mountain sheep.

Big Sandy Creek, in Kiowa County, is infamous as the site where Arapaho and Cheyenne Indians were massacred in 1864 by Colorado troops under Colonel John M. Chivington; the incident is usually called the "Sand Creek Massacre."

Big Thompson River, in Larimer and Weld counties, arises in Rocky Mountain National Park. Both this stream and the nearby Little Thompson River may have been named for English fur trapper David Thompson (1770–1857), employed in 1810 by the Northwest Fur Company to explore the Rockies.

Bijou [bē′ jōō] is the name of localities in Elbert and Morgan counties, as well as **Bijou Creek,** in Adams County. It seems to be from French *bijou* "jewel." However, the creek's name is said to reflect a misspelling of the name of Joseph Bijeau, a French guide who accompanied the expedition of Major Stephen H. Long in 1820.

Bisonte [bi sōn′ tē], in Baca County, is a Spanish word for the bison or American buffalo (*Bison bison*). However, the traditional word for "bison" in the Spanish of New Mexico and Colorado is masc. *cíbolo,* fem. *cíbola,* from *vaca de Cíbola,* literally "cow of Cibola." The fabled "Seven Cities of Cibola," for which the Spanish searched in vain, in fact took their name from *Shiwina,* the Zuni name for their pueblo in New Mexico.

Black is a term appearing in many place names, perhaps derived in some cases from a family name, but in other cases referring to dark color. **Black Canyon** is the name of nine geographical features in Colorado. The most famous is that of the Gunnison River in Montrose County; it constitutes the **Black Canyon of the Gunnison National Monument,** so called because of the gloom that shrouds the deep canyon most of the day. **Black Forest,** a community in El Paso County (est. 1866?, pop. 8,143), is named for the surrounding wooded area. The name recalls the Black Forest in Germany and refers to the huge stands of ponderosa pine trees, which sparked a timber industry in the 1870s.

Black Hawk, town on Colorado 119, in Gilpin County (est. 1859, inc. 1864, pop. 227). An early mining company brought into the area a quartz mill named after Black Hawk (1767–1838), a chief of the Sauk and Fox Indians in Illinois and Wisconsin. The name of the town is sometimes written as one word, Blackhawk.

Black Lake is the name of seven bodies of water in the state; one is in Rocky Mountain National Park, Larimer County. **Black Mountain** is the name of seventeen peaks in Colorado; the highest is in Hinsdale County (11,858 ft.). **Black Sage Pass,** in Gunnison County (9,745 ft.), is named for a variety of the sage plant.

Blaine, Mount, in Park County (12,303 ft.), was named for the American politician James G. Blaine (1830–93), who was a Republican candidate for president in 1884. A lower mountain of the same name is in Garfield County.

Blakeland, in Arapahoe County (est. 1919?), was named by Mrs. Mary N. Blake, who operated the Blakeland Poultry Farms.

Blanca [blang′ kə], town on U.S. 160 in Costilla County (est. 1908, inc. 1910, pop. 272). The town was born of a land lottery; people in all parts of the country were sold small tracts, with the understanding they would be eligible for larger plots of ground. The site was named for its location at the foot of **Blanca Peak,** located where Alamosa, Costilla, and Huerfano counties meet (14,345 ft.). The mountain is named with the feminine form of the Spanish word for "white," as its crest is nearly always crowned with snow. This peak is the highest of the Sierra Blanca, the range which also includes Baldy, Little Bear, Middle Creek, and Twin Peaks.

Blende [blend], on U.S. 50 in Pueblo County, was named for "zinc blende," also called sphalerite or zinc sulfide, a principal ore of zinc.

Bloom, on U.S. 350 in Otero County, was named for Frank G. Bloom, son-in-law of M. D. Thatcher, Sr.; Bloom operated cattle ranches owned by Thatcher.

Blue, occurring in many place names, often refers to the clear color of water or the smoky color of mountains. **Blue Mesa,** in Gunnison County, was named for the bluish appearance of sage growing on it. **Blue Mountain** is on U.S. 40 in Moffat County; the post office was moved here in 1950 from Skull Creek, where it had been established in 1929. **Blue River** is a stream in Grand and Summit counties; it gives its name to a town on Colorado 9 in Summit County (est. 1964, inc. 1964, pop. 440).

Boettcher [bech´ ər], in Larimer County, was named for Charles Boettcher, a pioneer Colorado industrialist. **Boettcher Lake** is in Jackson County.

Boggsville, in Bent County, once a center of the cattle industry, was named for Thomas Boggs.

Bonanza City, a town in Saguache County (est. 1880, inc. 1881, pop. 16). Bonanza is a Spanish word meaning "prosperity," and in mining days often referred to a rich body of ore. Only a few valuable claims were found in the Bonanza area, however, and the population—once up to thirteen hundred—drifted away after 1882.

Boncarbo [bon kär´ bō], in Las Animas County (est. 1915). Sometimes written as Bon Carbo, the name is a corruption of French *bon charbon* "good coal." The name was given by Abe Thompson, an official of the American Smelting and Refining Company, about 1915. A post office was established in 1917.

Bond, on Colorado 131 in Eagle County (est. 1934). Named for the rail link made here, connecting the Denver and Rio Grande Western Railroad main line to the Denver and Salt Lake Railroad. The connection shortened the rail distance between Denver and Salt Lake City by 173 miles.

Bondad [bon´ dad], on U.S. 550 in La Plata County, is Spanish for "goodness." However, a local tradition claims that the site was named after a family called Bonds.

Bonita [bō nē´ tə], in Saguache County, is from Spanish *bonita,* feminine of *bonito* "pretty." The same word appears in **Bonita Peak,** in San Juan County (13,286 ft.). The corresponding masculine form is found in **Bonito Mountain,** in Rio Grande County (12,181 ft.).

Book Cliffs is the name of geological formations in both Garfield and Mesa counties. Eroded hills of sandstone rise above one another in layers, like stacks of books.

Boone, town on Colorado 96 in Pueblo County (est. 1860, inc. 1956, pop. 341), was named by Colonel A. G. Boone, a great-grandson of the Kentucky pioneer Daniel Boone. Earlier it was known as Booneville and Boon Town.

Boreas [bōr′ ē əs] **Mountain,** in Park County (13,082 ft.), and **Boreas Pass,** on the Continental Divide between Summit and Park counties (11,481 ft.), bear the Greek name of the north wind.

Borrego [bə rā′ gō] **Canyon,** in Las Animas County, is from a Spanish word for "sheep."

Boulder, city located on **Boulder Creek** and on U.S. 36 (est. 1859, inc. 1871, pop. 83,312). Gold seekers came here in the fall of 1858; the settlement grew to supply miners in the mountains to the west. The name comes from the abundance of large rocks in the vicinity. The city is the seat of **Boulder County** (est. 1861, area 748 sq. mi., pop. 225,339). This was one of the original seventeen territorial counties named after the city; it is one of three which still has its original boundaries. Strangers to the state often confuse the name of the Colorado city with the names of Boulder Dam and Boulder City, which coincidentally lie on the Colorado River in the state of Nevada. Independently named is **Boulder Mountain** in Chaffee County (13,524 ft.).

Bountiful, on U.S. 285 in Conejos County, is named for an ancient city mentioned in the Book of Mormon; a town in Utah bears the same name.

Bovina [bō vē′ nə], on U.S. 24 in Lincoln County, is the Spanish word for "bovine," applied because of the cattle raising in the area.

Bowen [bō′ ən] **Mountain,** in Grand County (12,524 ft.), was named for James H. Bourn, who prospected here in 1875; his name was misinterpreted by a county clerk.

Bowie [bō′ ē], on Colorado 133 in Delta County (est. 1907), was orginally a coal camp called Reading, but the name was changed when a post office was established. The name honored Alexander Bowie, a native of

Scotland who in 1906 became part owner and general manager of the Juanita Coal & Coke Company here. After his death in 1917, the mine was operated by his descendants until the early 1970s.

Bow Mar [bō´ mär], town in Arapahoe and Jefferson counties (est. 1958, inc. 1958, pop. 854). Coined from the names of nearby Bowles and Marston lakes.

Box Canyon is a term describing a kind of canyon with steep vertical walls on three sides. There are seventeen places so named in Colorado.

Boyero [boi yâr´ ō], in Lincoln County (est. 1870), is Spanish for "ox-driver," also used locally to mean "bull pen." A town plat was filed in 1908 on part of the land of the first homesteader, Dr. C. A. Kelsey.

Brainard Lake, in Boulder County, was named for Colonel Wesley Brainard.

Brandon, on Colorado 96 in Kiowa County (est. 1887?), was probably named for a nearby reservoir, Lake Brandon; however, the origin of the lake's name is not known. This was one in a series of towns on the Missouri Pacific Railroad which were named alphabetically from east to west: Arden, Brandon, Chivington, etc.

Branson, town in Las Animas County (est. 1916, inc. 1921, pop. 58), was named for Al Branson of Trinidad, who was active in founding the settlement. At various times it was known as Wilson, Wilson Switch, and Coloflats. Under the name Coloflats, a post office was established in 1915.

Breckenridge, town on Colorado 9, (est. 1859, inc. 1880, pop. 1,285), and seat of Summit County. Founded by a party of prospectors under General George E. Spencer of Alabama. He named the town in honor of John Cabell Breckinridge (1821–75), a Kentuckian who was then U.S. Vice President. The gesture was intended to prompt Congress to create a post office for the new settlement; and it did. But because of Breckinridge's subsequent allegiance to the Confederacy, the citizens—ardent Unionists—petitioned Congress to change the name of the town. Accordingly, the first "i" was changed to "e," the spelling of the present form.

Breen, on Colorado 140 in La Plata County, is on the Southern Ute Indian Reservation (est. 1900). It was named for Dr. Thomas Breen, superintendent of the Fort Lewis Indian School in 1900.

Bridal Veil Falls, in San Miguel County, is the highest falls in the state at over 350 feet. Another falls with this name is in Rocky Mountain National Park, in Larimer County.

Briggsdale, on Colorado 14 in Weld County (est. 1909), was named for Frank M. Briggs, a farmer and real estate dealer who helped plat the townsite.

Brighton, city on U.S. 85 (est. 1882, inc. 1887, pop. 14,203), seat of Adams County. Named for Brighton, Massachusetts, home town of Mrs. D. F. Carmichael, wife of the man who laid out the town. Originally it was known as Hughes Junction, for General Bela M. Hughes, who came to Colorado in 1861 as president of the Overland Mail Company.

Bristol, on Colorado 196 in Prowers County (est. 1906), was named for C. H. Bristol, an official of the Santa Fe Railroad who also owned land in the vicinity. Supposedly Bristol's name was to have been given to the unincorporated town of Lancaster (now Hartman). Because of an error, the names were given to the "wrong towns."

Broadmoor, on Colorado 122 in El Paso County (est. 1890), named for the sweeping terrain of the area. The Broadmoor Land & Investment Company was headed by Count James Pourtales who, in 1891, opened a casino in the tract. Spencer Penrose's new Broadmoor Hotel formally opened on the same site in 1918.

Brook, referring to a small stream, occurs in several Colorado place names. **Brook Forest** is on the border of Jefferson and Clear Creek counties.

Broomfield, city on U.S. 287 in Adams, Boulder, and Jefferson counties (est. 1887, inc. 1961, pop. 24,638). Originally known as Zang's Spur, for Philip Zang, Denver businessman and brewer, who bred Percheron horses nearby. When the Denver and Salt Lake Railroad established a station here, the present name was adopted. Railroad officials noticed a small field of broom corn nearby, and suggested the name Broomfield.

Bross, Mount, in Park County (14,172 ft.), is named for William Bross (1813–89), Lieutenant Governor of Illinois, who owned mining property near Alma, Colorado. Writer Samuel Bowles and Bross together climbed Grays Peak and Mount Lincoln in 1868.

Brown is part of many Colorado place names; it may be either a color term or a family name. **Brown Mountain** is in Ouray County (13,330 ft.). The form "Browns" is more likely to reflect the family name, as in **Browns Peak,** in Chaffee County (13,523 ft.).

Brush, city on U.S. 34 in Morgan County (est. 1882, inc. 1884, pop. 4,165), was named for Jared L. Brush, a pioneer cattleman of the South Platte Valley. Long before the town was established, the site was a favorite shipping point on the old Texas–Montana cattle trail, and was known among cattlemen as Beaver Creek.

Brush Creek is the name of thirteen streams in Colorado; most were probably named for their dense vegetation, rather than for any individual named Brush. **Brush Hollow Creek** and **Reservoir** are in Fremont County.

Bryant, Mount, in Rocky Mountain National Park, Grand County (11,034 ft.), was named for William H. Bryant, first commodore of the Grand Lake Yacht Club in 1901.

Buck, referring to a male deer, has been used for the name of nine streams called **Buck Creek** and five summits called **Buck Mountain;** the highest of the latter is in Jackson County (11,396 ft.).

Buckingham, on Colorado 14 in Weld County (est. 1888), was named for C. D. Buckingham, superintendent of the McCook division of the Burlington Railroad, who surveyed and platted the townsite.

Buckley Air National Guard Base, in Arapahoe County, is named for Lieutenant John Harold Buckley, a Colorado veteran of World War I.

Buena Vista [byoo′ nə vis′ tə], town on the Arkansas River and U.S. 24, in Chaffee County (est. 1879, inc. 1879, pop. 1,752). The name represents the Spanish for "good view." A more authentic Spanish pronunciation would be something like [bwā′ nä vēs′ tä].

Buffalo refers to the bison (*Bison bison*); eight streams are called **Buffalo Creek** in Colorado, and the community of **Buffalo Creek,** in Jefferson County (est. 1877?), is named for one of these. Some such places may be named for eastern American cities such as Buffalo, New York. Colorado has two prominences called **Buffalo Mountain** (the higher in Summit County, 12,777 ft.), and two called **Buffalo Peak** (the higher in La Plata County, 12,728 ft.).

Buford [byoo′ fərd], in Rio Blanco County (est. 1890), was named for a "Colonel Buford," who served as a guide for Theodore Roosevelt on a hunting trip in the area.

Buick, in Elbert County, was named for a pioneer family; the name was originally written as Beuck.

Bull, in place names, is as likely to refer to the male buffalo as to the domestic bull. There are six streams called **Bull Creek** in the state, plus eight called **Bull Gulch.** Three peaks are called **Bull Mountain;** the highest is in Laramie County (10,082 ft.). **Bull Hill** (13,761 ft.) is a sub-peak of Mount Elbert.

Burlington, city on U.S. 24 (est. 1887, inc. 1888, pop. 2,941); seat of Kit Carson County. The first settlement here, in 1886, was platted and named Lowell. The plat was later abandoned, but a new one covering the same land was filed. The original town was moved to the site in 1887, and called Burlington, perhaps because many of the residents came from Burlington, Kansas.

Burns, on the Colorado River in Eagle County (post office est. 1895), was named for Jack Burns, a trapper who built his cabin here, and died in 1891.

Burro, referring to an animal frequently employed by early prospectors, is a common term in place names. The state has four streams called **Burro Creek,** and three peaks called **Burro Mountain;** the highest is in Rio Grande County (12,110 ft.).

Bustos [boos′ tōs] **Canyon,** in Pueblo County, is probably from a Spanish family name.

Buttes [byoots], on U.S. 85 and 87 in El Paso County. The term "butte" refers to a steep elevation, and is used in many other place names, such as Crested Butte.

Byers [bī′ ərz], community on U.S. 36, 40, and 287 in Arapahoe County (est. 1868, pop. 1,065). It was founded by a scout named Oliver P. Wiggins, and first called Bijou. Later it was renamed for William N. Byers, founder (in 1859) and publisher of the state's oldest newspaper, the *Rocky Mountain News* of Denver. His name was also given to **Byers Peak,** in Grand County (12,804 ft.).

Cabezon [kab´ ə zon] **Canyon,** in Archuleta County, is from Spanish *cabezón* "big head."

Cache [kash] refers to a hiding place for food or supplies (from French *cacher* "to hide"). The word occurs in a variety of Colorado names; thus **Cache Creek** is the name of three streams. The **Cache la Poudre** [kash´ lə po͞o´ dər] **River,** in Larimer County, was named by French-speaking Creole fur trappers from St. Louis; caught in an early fall snowstorm in 1836, they dug a hole beside a stream, not far from present Bellvue, in which they deposited some of their supplies, including gunpowder. The next spring they found their cache intact. The river is commonly referred to as "The Poudre" [po͞o´ dər]. The name of **La Poudre Pass** also comes from this source.

Caddoa [kə do͞o´ ə], in Bent County (est. 1863); also pronounced [kad´ o͞o]. Probably named after the Caddo Indian tribe, now living in Oklahoma. The English term is abbreviated from the native name *kaduhdáachu'.*

Cahone [kə ho͞on´], on U.S. 666 in Dolores County (est. 1912?), is from Spanish *cajón* "box," in this case referring to a box canyon. Named by the first postmaster, Bert Ballenger.

Calcite [kal´ sīt], on Howard Creek in Fremont County, refers to the mineral calcium carbonate, found in the limestone which was quarried here.

Calhan [kal´ ən], town on U.S. 24 in El Paso County (est. 1888, inc. 1919, pop. 562). Founded as a railroad watertank station because good water was available at shallow depth from Big Sandy Creek. Originally named Calahan for a contractor who built this section of the Chicago, Rock Island and Pacific Railroad. The railroad's timetables shortened the name to its present form.

Calumet [kal´ yə met], on Colorado 69 in Huerfano County. A French word for the ceremonial pipe used by Indians, the "peace pipe."

Cameo [kam´ ē o͞o], in Mesa County (est. 1907), refers to the outline of a stone formation on the face of a cliff overlooking the settlement. John McNeil, president of the Grand Junction Fuel & Mining Company, opened the Cameo Coal Mine and founded the town.

Cameron Pass, between Jackson and Larimer counties (10,276 ft.), was named for General Robert A. Cameron, the founder of Fort Collins. **Mount Cameron** is in Park County (14,239 ft.).

Camp Amache [ä mä′ chē], also written as Campamanche, in Prowers County. The site of Amache Relocation Center, where Japanese-Americans were interned during World War II, is said to be named for Amache, the daughter of Ochinee (Lone Wolf), a Cheyenne chief. In 1861, at the age of fifteen, she married John Wesley Prowers, a cattleman; Prowers County is named after him.

Camp Bird, in Ouray County (est. 1896). Named for the famous Camp Bird Gold Mine. Originally a silver claim, the mine produced almost four million dollars in six years (between 1896 and 1902). The name refers to a bird which frequents mining camps, the Rocky Mountain or Canada Jay, *Perisoreus canadensis* —also called the "whiskey jack."

Camp Hale, on U.S. 24 in Eagle County, was named for Brigadier General Irving Hale of Denver, a hero of the Spanish-American War.

Campion [kam′ pē ən], on Colorado 60 in Larimer County (est. 1907, pop. 1,692), was named for John F. Campion, who made a fortune from mining in Leadville. The town was settled by Seventh Day Adventists who started the Campion Academy, a coeducational boarding school.

Campo [kam′ pō], a town on U.S. 287 and 385, in Baca County (est. 1912, inc. 1950, pop. 121). The name is Spanish for "field."

Canadian River is the name of two streams in Colorado. One—a tributary of the North Platte River, in Jackson County—is said to have been named by James Pinkham and August Speck, the earliest inhabitants of the North Park area, and perhaps referred to the presence of Canadian trappers. But another Canadian River rises in Las Animas County, flowing into New Mexico, Texas, and Oklahoma, where it joins the Arkansas River. Its name seems to be an adaptation of Spanish *Río Canadiano,* a folk etymology from Caddo *káyántinu',* a name not for the Canadian River but for the nearby Red River.

Canfield, in Boulder County, was named for Ike Canfield, a coal mine operator.

Cannibal Plateau, in Gunnison County, was named after Alferd [sic] Packer, who in 1874 killed and ate five companions. A cafeteria used by students at the University of Colorado, Boulder, is now called the Alferd Packer Grill.

Canon [kan´ yən], also spelled Canyon, from Spanish *cañón,* occurs in many Colorado place names; thus there are eight streams in the state called **Canyon Creek.** A place called simply **Canon** exists in Conejos County. **Canon City,** on U.S. 50, is the seat of Fremont County (est. 1859, inc. 1872, pop. 12,576); its name is derived from the nearby Grand Canyon of the Arkansas River. The site was a camping ground for Zebulon Pike in 1806, and is now the location of the Colorado State Penitentiary.

Canoncito [kan yən sē´ tō], in Las Animas County, represents Spanish *cañoncito* "little canyon."

Canon Pintado [pin tä´ dō], in Rio Blanco County, represents Spanish *Cañón Pintado* "painted canyon," the name given by Fathers Dominguez and Escalante on their 1776 expedition, because of the pictographs left here by the prehistoric Indian culture. **Canyon Diablo** [dē ä´ blō] is the name of two canyons in Colorado; the name represents Spanish *Cañón (del) Diablo* "devil's canyon." **Canyon Infierno** [in fē âr´ nō], also written "Inferno," is in Hinsdale County, from Spanish *Cañón (del) Infierno* "Hell Canyon."

Capitol City, on Henson Creek in Hinsdale County, was named by early residents in 1877, in hope that it would become the capitol of Colorado. **Capitol Peak,** in Pitkin County (14,130 ft.), was named for its stately form by the Hayden Survey. Capitol and Snowmass peaks were earlier called the "Twins," or Capitol Peak and Whitehouse Peak, for the two well-known buildings in Washington, D.C.

Capulin [kap yo͞o lēn´], on Colorado 15 in Conejos County (est. 1867); also pronounced [kap yo͞o´ lin]. The name is Mexican Spanish for the "choke-cherry" or wild cherry, *Prunus virginiana*; Spanish borrowed the term from Aztec *capolin.*

Carbon, occurring in many Colorado place names, usually reflects Spanish *carbón,* meaning both "charcoal" and "(mineral) coal." **Carbon Peak** is in Gunnison County (12,709 ft.).

Carbonera [kär bə när´ ə], in Garfield County, is Spanish for "coal mine."

Carbonate Mountain is in Chaffee County (12,944 ft.). There are also three summits called **Carbonate Hill,** the highest being in Gunnison County (12,713 ft.).

Carbondale [kär′ bən dāl], town on Colorado 133 in Garfield County (est. 1883, inc. 1888, pop. 3,004). Named by John Mankin, one of the founders, for his home town in Pennsylvania.

Cardiff, on Colorado 82 in Garfield County, was named after the city in Wales.

Caribou [kâr′ i boo], in Boulder County, is a name for the northern reindeer, not found in Colorado. The mining settlement in Boulder County was named in 1869 by a miner, George Lytle, after the Cariboo Mountains of Alberta, Canada.

Carlton, on U.S. 50 and 385, in Prowers County (est. 1886), was originally listed as Conroe and Grote. The town site was platted by C. H. Frybarger of the Colorado Land & Title Company, but the source of the name is unknown.

Carnero [kär när′ ō] **Creek,** in Saguache County, contains the Spanish word for "sheep."

Carr, in Weld County (est. 1872?), was named for Robert E. Carr, an associate of former Territorial Governor John Evans. Carr later became president of the Kansas Pacific Railroad.

Carracas [kə rä′ kəs], in Archuleta County. Spanish dictionaries list this word as meaning "rattle, instrument used instead of bells on the last three days of Holy Week"; also a type of sailing ship. Or is this a misspelling of Caracas in Venezuela?

Cascade, on U.S. 24 in El Paso County (est. 1886; with the adjacent community of Chipita Park, the population is 1,479). Named for the many beautiful waterfalls in the surrounding canyon streams. In 1889 the Pikes Peak carriage road was built from this point, a toll road to the top of the 14,110-foot mountain. **Cascade Creek** is the name of eleven streams in Colorado.

Castle Peak, in Gunnison and Pitkin counties (14,265 ft.), was named by the Hayden Survey; the noticable "towers" along its ridges resembled the outline of a European castle.

Castle Rock, city on U.S. 85 and 87, seat of Douglas County (est. 1874, inc. 1881, pop. 8,708). Named for the nearby castellated rock formation, which in turn was named by Dr. Edwin James, the botanist of Major Stephen

Long's expedition of 1820. The name is also applied to fifteen other prominences in the state; the highest is in Gunnison County (11,204 ft.).

Cebolla [sə voi′ ə] **Creek,** in Hinsdale and Gunnison counties, contains the Spanish word for "onion," perhaps referring to wild species of the area (*Allium textile* or *Allium geyeri*).

Cedar, referring to the red cedar (*Juniperus scopulorum*), occurs in many place names; it is applied to a settlement in San Miguel County. There are eight streams called **Cedar Creek** in the state. **Cedaredge** is a town on Colorado 65 in Delta County (est. 1882, inc. 1907, pop. 1,380). **Cedarwood** is a locale in Pueblo County (est. 1912); it was founded as a station on the Colorado and Southern Railroad, and was named by the Reverend J. H. White.

Cement Creek, in Gunnison County, is said to have been named for conglomerate outcroppings, looking like poorly poured concrete.

Centennial, in Weld County (pop. 2,618 in 1973). Perhaps the most famous fictitious town in Colorado, the site of James A. Michener's best-selling novel *Centennial* (1974). Said by some to be modeled on the existing town of Keota. The name is derived from the term Centennial State, applied to Colorado because it was admitted to the Union in 1876, a hundred years after the Declaration of Independence. **Centennial Village** is a real place near Greeley, a historical site with reconstructed buildings and gardens; it was opened in 1976 to celebrate one hundred years of statehood. A non-fictitious **Centennial** also exists as a postal station in Englewood, Arapahoe County.

Center, town on Colorado 112 in Saguache County (est. 1898, inc. 1907, pop. 1,963). Founded and platted by J. L. Hunt, owner of the townsite land, and originally called Centerview. Later it was renamed by the postal authorities. Presumably the name was given because the town is in the central part of the San Luis Valley.

Central City, city and seat of Gilpin County (est. 1859, inc. 1864, pop. 335), founded as a trading center for miners in surrounding communities. *Rocky Mountain News* publisher William N. Byers suggested the name because of the town's hub location among the gold camps.

Cerro, a Spanish word for "hill, mountain," occurs in many place names; in Colorado English it is usually pronounced [sē′ rō]. **Cerro del Zopilote**

[sō pē lō′ tē], a peak in Archuleta County (7,924 ft.), means "Buzzard Peak." **Cerro Summit,** a pass in Montrose County (7,909 ft.), was used by the Spanish in the 1700s.

Chacra [chä′ krə], on U.S. 6 in Garfield County, is Spanish for "a rustic dwelling, a farm."

Chacuaco [chə kwä′ kō] **Creek,** also spelled Chiquaqua or Chaquaqua, is in Las Animas County. In the Spanish of New Mexico and Colorado, the term means "elderberry."

Chaffee [chä′ fē] **County** (est. 1879, area 1,038 sq. mi., pop. 12,684), was named in honor of Senator Jerome B. Chaffee (1825–86), who retired from the U.S. Senate in the year the county was created from a part of Lake County. The county seat is Salida.

Chama [chä′ mə], on Culebra Creek in Costilla County (est. 1860), was named after Chama, New Mexico, about eight miles south of the Colorado border. The New Mexican name reflects a place name *tzama* in the Tewa Indian language, said to mean "here they have wrestled." There is another Chama in Huerfano County. **Chama Peak** is in Archuleta County (12,019 ft.).

Chambers Lake, in Larimer County, was named for Robert Chambers, a trapper killed here by Indians in the early 1850s.

Chance, in Gunnison County (est. 1894), is said to have been suggested by the first miners for "the luck of the camp."

Chapin [chä′ pin], **Mount,** in Rocky Mountain National Park, Larimer County (12,454 ft.). Probably for Frederick Hastings Chapin of Hartford, Connecticut, who came to climb in the Rockies in 1886 to 1888.

Chautauqua [shə tô′ kwə] **Park,** a recreational facility in the city of Boulder. It takes its name from the organization of educational and cultural centers by which it was founded in the late nineteenth century, originating in Lake Chautauqua, New York. The name is of Iroquois Indian origin.

Chattanooga [chat ə nōō′ gə], on U.S. 550 in San Juan County (est. 1883), is named for the city in Tennessee. The word is said to mean "rock rising to a point" in the Creek Indian language.

Chemung [chə mung′], in Cheyenne County, is named for a town in New York State, said to mean "big horn" in an Algonkian Indian language.

Cheney [chē′ nē] **Center,** in Prowers County (est. 1886?). For Cheney Center, Kansas, which suggests the first settlers came from that town. The Kansas community, in turn, was named for B. P. Cheney, a stockholder of the Atchison, Topeka and Santa Fe Railroad.

Cheraw [châr ô′], town on Colorado 109 in Otero County (est. 1907, inc. 1917, pop. 265). Named for a nearby lake, which derived its name from the Cheraw Indians—a tribe of the Siouan family, originally living in Virginia and the Carolinas.

Cherokee [châr′ ō kē] **Park,** in Larimer County. After the original Cherokee Indian territory in Georgia was confiscated by the U.S. government in the 1830s, a party of Indians are said to have traveled to the Pacific Coast to look for a new home. On the return trip through Colorado, they supposedly camped in this location. A Cherokee Nation was eventually established not on the West Coast, but in Oklahoma.

Cherry is a common term in Colorado place names; in many cases it probably referred originally to the wild "choke cherry," *Prunus virginiana.* There are twelve streams named **Cherry Creek;** the most famous is the one which runs through the Denver area, and on which the city was founded. The community of **Cherry Creek** is in Arapahoe and Douglas counties. **Cherry Hills Village** is a city in Arapahoe County (est. 1870, inc. 1945, pop. 5,245), named for the large cherry orchards which were once in the area.

Cheyenne [shī an′] **County** (est. 1889, area 1,772 sq. mi., pop. 2,396). Named after the town which became the county seat, **Cheyenne Wells,** on U.S. 40 (est. 1870, inc. 1890, pop. 1,128). The county was created from portions of Elbert and Bent counties. The town's name was originally applied to a stage station, five miles north of the present site; that location was named for the Cheyenne Indians of the Great Plains, and for several wells that were dug there. "Cheyenne" is not the name used by the Cheyenne tribe for themselves; it is said to be a Sioux name, *Shairena,* meaning "people of alien speech." The Cheyenne tribe now has reservations in Montana and Oklahoma.

Chicago Creek and **Chicago Lake,** in Clear Creek County, are named for Chicago, Illinois; the name means "wild onion place" in an Algonkian Indian language. **Chicago Peak** is in Ouray County (13,385 ft.).

Chickaree is a name for the red squirrel or pine squirrel (*Tamiasciurus hudsonicus*); there is a **Chickaree Lake** in Rocky Mountain National Park, Grand County. The word "chickaree" is imitative of the squirrel's call.

Chicoso [chi kō′ sō] **Creek,** in Pueblo County. In the Spanish of New Mexico and Colorado, *chico* is a plant called "rabbit thorn." *Chicoso* is then "full of rabbit thorn."

Chief Hosa [hō′ sə], on U.S. 40 in Jefferson County, honors an Arapaho chief named *ho'sa,* meaning "little crow."

Chiefs Head Peak, in Rocky Mountain National Park, Boulder County (13,579 ft.), is said to reflect the Arapaho Indian name, which meant "head mountain"; some people saw in the peak the profile of an Indian head, complete with war bonnet.

Chimney is a term applied to many tall geological formations in Colorado; eight of these are called "Chimney Rock." The community of **Chimney Rock,** on Colorado 151, is in Archuleta County (est. 1880?). An earlier name was Dyke, referring to a type of rock wall.

Chipeta [chi pē′ tə], also written as **Chipita,** was the wife of the Ute Indian Chief Ouray. It is derived from Ute *chipít,* referring to water springing up, from the verb *chipí* "to move up or out." The name **Chipeta** is given to a settlement in Delta County; to **Chipeta Lakes,** to the south in Montrose County; to **Chipeta Mountain,** on the Continental Divide in Chaffee County (12,853 ft.); and (with a different spelling) to **Chipita Park,** on U.S. 24 in El Paso County (est. 1890), known until 1927 as Ute Park.

Chiquita [chi kē′ tə] **Mountain,** in Rocky Mountain National Park, Larimer County (13,069 ft.), was named for the heroine of a 1902 potboiling novel: *Chiquita, the Romance of a Ute Chief's Daughter.* There is possible confusion with Chipita, the name of the wife of Chief Ouray.

Chivington [chiv′ ing t'n], on Colorado 96 in Kiowa County (est. 1887); also pronounced [shiv′ ing t'n]. Named for Colonel John M. Chivington, a former minister, whose volunteer troops in 1864 engaged in a bloody battle with Indians at Big Sandy Creek, near the town's location. The incident is often referred to as the "Sand Creek Massacre."

Chromo [krō´ mō], on U.S. 84 in Archuleta County (est. 1881), was originally known as Price, for its first postmaster, Charles W. Price. The post office was discontinued and mail received at Durango. When application was later made for a new post office, authorities advised a new name to avoid confusion with Price, Utah. Charles Price is said to have suggested Chromo, as he had seen and named Chromo Mountain, New Mexico, many years before. The name is from Greek *chromos* "color," suitable for the vivid landscape in the vicinity.

Cimarron [sim ə rōn´], on U.S. 50 in Montrose County (est. 1875?). From the **Cimarron River** (Montrose and Gunnison counties) on which it is located, named in turn from Spanish *cimarrón* "wild, unruly," which is also applied to the "bighorn" or mountain sheep. **Cimarron Hills** is a community in El Paso County (pop. 11,160). There is a **Cimarron River** in Baca County. **Cimarrona** [sim ə rō´ nə] **Peak,** in Hinsdale County (12,536 ft.), represents the feminine form of the Spanish word.

Cinnamon, perhaps referring to reddish brown color, provides a name for two streams named **Cinnamon Creek,** and two peaks called **Cinnamon Mountain;** the higher is in San Juan County (13,328 ft.). **Cinnamon Pass** is between Hinsdale and San Juan counties (12,600 ft.).

Cirrus [sûr´ əs], **Mount,** on the Continental Divide between Jackson and Grand counties (12,797 ft.). The term refers to high, feathery clouds. This peak was named in 1914 by James Grafton Rogers, who also named other nearby mountains after cloud types: Mount Cumulus and Mount Nimbus.

Cisneros [siz när´ ōs] **Creek,** in Huerfano County, is a common Spanish family name, originally meaning "swan's nests."

Clark, in Routt County (post office est. 1889), was perhaps named for Worthington Clark, a stagecoacher of Walden, Colorado; or for Rufus Clark, who may have been the first postmaster. **Clark Peak,** in Larimer County (12,951 ft.), is named for William Clark (1770–1838) of the Lewis and Clark Expedition.

Clarkville, on Colorado 59 in Yuma County (est. 1933), was named for Ted Clark, who was appointed as the first postmaster in 1936.

Clear Creek is the name of fourteen streams in Colorado. One of these gave its name to **Clear Creek County** (est. 1861, area 394 sq. mi., pop. 7,619); the county seat is Georgetown. The creek was first called Vasquez Fork of the South Platte River, but the present name was adopted by 1860.

The county is one of the seventeen original territorial counties, and one of three which retain their original boundaries.

Clifford, on Big Sandy Creek in Lincoln County, was named for Billy Clifford, track foreman for the Kansas Pacific Railroad.

Clifton, on U.S. 6 in Mesa County (est. 1882, pop. 12,671), was named for the Book Cliffs which are near the Denver and Rio Grande Railroad at this point. The name was originally applied to a section of track, later to a station, and finally to a community.

Climax, on Colorado 91 in Lake County (est. 1917). Alternately called Fremont Pass and Climax, the latter because of its position near the Continental Divide. The name became official when a post office was established.

Coal, historically an important mineral product of Colorado, gives its name to eighteen streams called **Coal Creek.** One of these gave its name to **Coal Creek,** a town in Fremont County (est. 1872, inc. 1882, pop. 157). There are also three peaks in the state called **Coal Mountain;** the highest is in Gunnison County (11,705 ft.).

Coaldale, in Fremont County (est. 1884), was named for a coal mining camp, earlier called De Pauls. Later the town became a center of gypsum mining.

Coalmont, in Jackson County (est. 1911), named to suggest "coal mountain." The coal is so close to the surface here that there was an early strip-mining operation.

Cochetopa [kō chi tō´ pə] **Pass,** also written as Cochetopah or Chocetopa, is on the Continental Divide, in Saguache County (10,032 ft.); the pronunciation [koch i tō´ pə] is also reported. Also called North Pass. Probably from Ute *kuchúpupan* "buffalo passing," from *kuch* "buffalo." The pass was once an Indian and buffalo trail between the San Luis Valley and the Gunnison area. Nearby is **Cochetopa Dome** (11,132 ft.); **Cochetopa Creek** is in Gunnison County.

Cokedale, town on Colorado 12 in Las Animas County (est. 1906, inc. 1948, pop. 116). A station on the Denver and Rio Grande Railroad, and a coal mining community, with ovens to make coke.

Collbran [kōl´ bran], town on Colorado 330 in Mesa County (est. 1891, inc. 1908, pop. 228); also pronounced [kōl´ brən]. The site was originally named Hawhurst; but through the influence of Dr. Wallace de Beque, it was given the name of Collbran, a former railroad man in the community.

Collegiate Peaks, in Chaffee County, includes five peaks over fourteen thousand feet, named after universities: Mount Oxford, Mount Harvard, Mount Columbia, Mount Princeton, and Mount Yale. This pattern of naming was begun by Professor Josiah D. Whitney, first head of the Harvard Mining School, who surveyed this area in 1869; Mount Whitney in California was named for him.

Colona [kə lō′ nə], on U.S. 550 in Ouray County, was a term proposed as a name for the state in 1858; it was probably formed from Spanish *Colón* "Columbus," thus being a kind of equivalent of "Columbia." The name was adopted by the town in 1862; it had previously been called Hotchkiss, for Enos Hotchkiss.

Colorado [kol ə rad′ ō, kol ə rä′ dō]; old-fashioned pronunciations are [kol ə rä′ dō] and [kol ə rä′ də]. The state is named for the **Colorado River,** which rises in Grand County, and flows southwestward through Eagle, Garfield, and Mesa counties; it then continues through Utah and Arizona, forms the boundary between Arizona and California, and ends in Mexico, where it flows into the Gulf of California. The name was first given to the Arizona tributary now called the Little Colorado River; this was called *Río Colorado* "red river" by the Spanish explorer Juan de Oñate in 1605, because of the red muddy water, and the name was later extended to the main stream. Until the twentieth century, the name "Colorado River" was applied upstream only as far as the Green River, in Utah; the portion arising in Colorado was called the Grand River, so named by French trappers because of its size. (From this usage are derived such place names as Grand Junction, Grand Lake, and Grand County.)

When Colorado Territory was organized in 1861, the name was selected by Congress in recognition of the fact that the Colorado River had one of its sources in the Grand River. In subsequent years, as geographical nomenclature was regularized, the principle was established that a river should have a single name from its source to its mouth; and that, of two major tributaries, the name of the main river should be applied to the longer. Since the Green is longer than the Grand, this would have meant that the name "Colorado River" would be assigned to the Green River. In 1921, however, Congress decided that the name should instead be assigned to the Grand River of Colorado. When this was done, a stretch of some eighty miles of the Grand River remained in Utah with its name unchanged. After 1921 the Utah Legislature corrected this by changing the name of that stretch to the Colorado. **Colorado National Monument,** in Mesa County, is named for the river.

Colorado City, community on Colorado 165 in Pueblo County (est. 1963, pop. 1,149). The site was formerly Crow Junction, which, in the 1880s, boasted a post office. (The name should not be confused with an earlier Colorado City near Colorado Springs.)

Colorado Springs, city on U.S. 24, 85, and 87 (est. 1871, inc. 1886, pop. 281,140); seat of El Paso County. Laid out near the site of the older settlement of Colorado City, it takes its name from the numerous mineral springs in the area. For a time it was known as El Paso (Spanish for "the pass") because of its proximity to Ute Pass. General William J. Palmer, head of the Denver and Rio Grande Railroad, was the moving force in the Colorado Springs Company which organized the city.

Colorow [kəl ə rō´] **Mountain,** in Rio Blanco County (7,873 ft.), is named for a Ute Indian chief of Comanche origins, who was suspected of murdering Nathan Meeker, U.S. Indian agent at White River. In spite of these associations, the name Colorow is given to six features in various parts of the state.

Columbia, Mount, in Chaffee County (14,073 ft.), is a member of the Collegiate Group of peaks; it was one of the last named for a university. Roger W. Toll of Denver named it about 1916, and the name was adopted by the Colorado Mountain Club in 1922.

Columbine [kol´ əm bīn] refers to the Colorado blue columbine (*Aquilegia caerulea*), which has been the official state flower since 1899. There is a locale called **Columbine** in Routt County. There are also three streams in the state called **Columbine Creek,** and **Columbine Pass** is in Montrose County (9,120 ft.). **Columbine Valley** is a town on Colorado 75 in Arapahoe and Jefferson counties (pop. 23,969).

Comanche [kə man´ chē], in Adams County, bears the name of a major Indian tribe of the southern Plains. The name is from Spanish, which took it from Ute *kümmanchi* "stranger" or the like. **Comanche Peak** is in Larimer County (12,702 ft.).

Commerce City, a city on Colorado 2 in Adams County (pop. 16,466), was named for its industrial and commercial prospects.

Como [kō´ mō] and **Como Lake** are in Park County (an older pronunciation is [kō´ mə]). The name comes from Lake Como in Italy.

Conejos [kə nā´ əs], seat of Conejos County (est. 1855, pop. 428); also pronounced [kə nā´ hōs]. One of the oldest towns in the state, with the first church and first convent built in Colorado. The church, Our Lady of Guadalupe, was completed in 1859. Named for the **Conejos River,** so called by the Spaniards of New Mexico long before the permanent settlements of the region began. The word is Spanish for "rabbits." Also named for the river is **Conejos County** (est. 1861, area 1,268 sq. mi., pop. 7,453), of which the county seat is Conejos; this is one of the original territorial counties. **Conejos Peak** is also in the county (13,172 ft.).

Conifer, on U.S. 285 in Jefferson County (est. 1860), was named for the thick growth of evergreen trees in the area. It was first known as Hutchison, for early settler George Hutchison; and later as Junction City, changing to the present name in 1900.

Continental Divide, the dividing line between the Atlantic and Pacific watersheds. The divide runs for nearly seven hundred miles, roughly from north to south, through central Colorado.

Conundrum Creek, in Pitkin County; also **Conundrum Peak** (14,022 ft.). The term refers to a puzzle or riddle. Colorado also has places called Paradox and Quandary; perhaps some of these refer to locations where early travelers lost their way.

Cony [kō´ nē] **Lake,** in Boulder County, is named for a small animal of the high peak country, also called the pika (*Ochotona princeps*).

Cope, on U.S. 36 in Washington County (est. 1888), was named for its founder, Jonathan C. Cope, an employee of the Burlington Railroad. Cope was sent to take a homestead that would serve as a rail terminal for a projected line, and the settlement grew around his ranch house. However, the post office was first known as Gray.

Copeland Mountain, in Boulder County (13,176 ft.), was named after John B. Copeland, who homesteaded nearby in 1896.

Copper, an important mineral product of Colorado, gives its name to many places. Five peaks are called **Copper Mountain,** the highest in Mineral County (11,954 ft.). One of these gave its name to the locality of **Copper Mountain** in Summit County (12,441 ft.).

Cordova [kōr′ də və] **Pass,** between Huerfano and Las Animas counties (11,743 ft.); the English pronunciation [kōr dō′ və] also occurs. A Spanish surname; originally the name of a famous city in Spain, now spelled *Córdoba.*

Cornish, on Colorado 392 in Weld County (est. 1911), was named for a Mr. Cornish, a civil engineer of the Union Pacific Railroad. The site was laid out by Henry Breder, owner of the land, when the railroad built a branch through the area, from Greeley to Briggsdale.

Corona [kə rō′ nə], **The,** a summit in Las Animas County (6,823 ft.). The word is Spanish or Latin for "crown." **Corona Pass** (11,670 ft.) in Boulder County is the railroad name for Rollins Pass.

Corral [kə ral′] **Creek** is the name of thirteen streams in Colorado. The Spanish term means "fence" or "enclosure."

Cortez [kōr tez′], city on U.S. 160 and 666 (est. 1886, inc. 1902, pop. 7,284); also pronounced [kōr′ tez]. The seat of Montezuma County, named for the Spanish conquistador who conquered Mexico in the sixteenth century. The name was not applied in Colorado by the Spanish, but was suggested by James W. Hanna, homesteader, who sold the site to the Montezuma Land & Development Company.

Cory, on Colorado 65 in Delta County, was named for Cora Harshman, wife of the first postmaster.

Costilla [kos tē′ yə] **County** (est. 1861, area 1,213 sq. mi., pop. 3,190). The county seat is San Luis. Along with the town of Costilla, New Mexico, just across the state line, the county was named for the **Costilla River,** so called before 1800. The Spanish name means "rib," but in New Mexico can also refer to the slope of a mountain range. One of Colorado Territory's original counties.

Cotopaxi [kō tō pak′ sē], on U.S. 50 in Fremont County (est. 1873?), was named for Mount Cotopaxi in Ecuador, at 19,347 feet the world's highest active volcano. Its name is said to be from the Quichua Indian language, meaning "shining pile." The name was applied in Colorado by Emanuel Saltiel, the owner of a silver mine, who brought a Jewish agricultural colony here in 1882.

Cottonwood is the name of a tree, especially the narrowleaf cottonwood (*Populus angustifolia*). It has given its name to many places in Colorado, including twenty-eight streams called **Cottonwood Creek,** and thirteen called **Cottonwood Gulch.** There is a **Cottonwood Pass,** between Gunnison and Chaffee counties (12,126 ft.), and a **Cottonwood Peak** in Eagle County (11,477 ft.).

Cow is a term occurring in many Colorado place names; it may sometimes refer to the female buffalo, rather than to the domestic bovine. Twelve streams are called **Cow Creek,** and **Cow Mountain** is in Teller County (11,143 ft.). There are also six geographical features called **Cow Canyon,** four called **Cow Gulch,** and two called **Cow Lake** in various parts of the state.

Cowdrey [kou′ drē], on Colorado 125 in Jackson County (est. 1882), was named for an early settler, Charles Cowdrey, who established a hotel or roadhouse in the village.

Coyote [kī′ ōt], as the name of an animal (*Canis latrans*) related to the dog and wolf, is borrowed from Spanish, which takes it in turn from Aztec *coyotl.* The state has five streams called **Coyote Creek.** In some other parts of the U.S., the word is pronounced [kī ō′ tē].

Cragmor, in El Paso County, is intended to suggest the meeting of mountains and plains.

Craig, city on U.S. 40 (est. 1889, inc. 1908, pop. 8,091); seat of Moffat County. From the name of the promoter, the Reverend Bayard Craig, who laid out the plan for his Craig Townsite Company. Settlement began earlier when ranch claims were developed. **Mount Craig,** in Grand County (12,007 ft.), is named for the same person. There is also a **Craig Peak** in Eagle County (11,902 ft.).

Crawford, town on Colorado 92 in Delta County (est. 1882, inc. 1910, pop. 221), was named for George A. Crawford—frontier capitalist, speculator, and former governor of Kansas, who started many towns on Colorado's western slope in the 1880s.

Creede [krēd], town on Colorado 149 (est. 1890, inc. 1892, pop. 362); seat of Mineral County. Nicholas C. Creede discovered the Amethyst Lode near here, and almost overnight the influx of miners and others swelled the population to ten thousand. The town of Creede absorbed several camps in its rapid growth, including Amethyst, Jimtown, and Bachelor. Jesse James's killer, Bob Ford, met his end here, and poet Cy Warman immortalized the town with these lines: "It's day all day in the daytime, and there is no night in Creede."

Crested Butte [byo͞ot′], town on Colorado 135 in Gunnison County (est. 1879, inc. 1880, pop. 878). Named for the nearby mountain (12,162 ft.), the top of which resembles a cock's comb or a helmet. The town was founded by Howard F. Smith, who brought the first saw mill here. The nearby ski area constitutes the town of **Mount Crested Butte** (est. 1974, inc. 1974, pop. 274).

Crestone [kres tōn′], town in Saguache County (est. 1879, inc. 1902, pop. 39). Founded by gold prospectors, the town takes its name from the nearby Crestone group of peaks, named in turn from Spanish *crestón* "cock's comb." The peaks are **Crestone Needle,** in Custer County (14,197 ft.); **Crestone Peak,** in Custer and Saguache counties (14,294 ft.); and Kit Carson Mountain.

Cripple Creek, city on Colorado 67 (est. 1891, inc. 1892, pop. 584); seat of Teller County. From a stream, Cripple Creek, named by early cowboys because a cow was crippled attempting to cross it. The site was first homesteaded in 1876 by William W. Womack of Kentucky. Later, "Bob" Womack, son of the original owner, prospected for gold here. His assays of ore brought many miners to the area, and a mining camp called Fremont soon mushroomed. The name was changed to its present one after a town was platted; it is known as one of the great gold camps of the early West.

Critchell [krich′ əl], in Jefferson County, was named for the first postmaster.

Crook, town on U.S. 138 in Logan County (est. 1881, inc. 1918, pop. 148), was named by the Union Pacific Railroad after Major General George R. Crook, who commanded the military Department of the Platte from 1875 to 1882.

Cross Mountain, on U.S. 40 in Moffat County, was named for the mountain just to the north, supposedly so called because a large cross made of white quartz or granite was found on its top.

Crowley [krō′ lē], town on Colorado 96 (est. 1880, inc. 1921, pop. 225). Located in **Crowley County** (est. 1911, area 802 sq. mi., pop. 3,946). The county seat is not Crowley, but Ordway. Town and county are named for John H. Crowley, a state senator from Otero County at the time when that county was divided to form Crowley County.

Crystal, in Gunnison County. The term occurs in many other place names; thus ten streams in the state are called **Crystal Creek,** and four mountains are called **Crystal Peak;** the highest is in Summit County (13,852 ft.). **Crystal River** is in Gunnison, Pitkin, and Garfield counties.

Cuates [kwä′ tās] **Creek,** a stream in Costilla County. In Mexican Spanish, *cuate* means "twin, companion," borrowed from Aztec *coatl* "twin."

Cuchara [kōo chä′ rə], on Colorado 12 in Huerfano County (est. 1916); also pronounced [kōo chär′ ə]. Named for the **Cucharas River** (Spanish *cuchara* "spoon," plural *cucharas*), which in turn derived its name from the spoon-like shape of the valley through which it flows. A post office at Cuchara Camps was moved to the present site in 1957. Another, earlier site called Cucharas, northeast of Walsenburg (and sometimes spelled Cacharas), also on the river, was prominent in the early 1870s. **Cucharas Pass** is between Huerfano and Las Animas counties (9,941 ft.).

Cuchilla Alta [kōo chē′ yə äl′ tə], is a ridge in Costilla County. In the Spanish of New Mexico and Colorado, *cuchilla* refers to a ridge or cliff; *alta* means "high."

Cuerna Verde [kwâr′ nə vâr′ dē] **Park,** in Pueblo County, contains a garbling of Spanish *Cuerno Verde* "green horn," the name of a Comanche chief killed near here in 1779. His name is also reflected in that of nearby Greenhorn Mountain.

Culebra [koo lā′ brə] **Peak,** in Costilla County (14,047 ft.); an old-fashioned pronunciation is [kyōo lē′ brə]. The word in Spanish means "snake," but here it refers to winding **Culebra Creek,** a tributary of the Rio Grande. This is an early name, appearing as "Rio de la Culebra" on Lieutenant Pike's map of 1810.

Cumberland Pass, in Gunnison County (12,000 ft.), may have been named for Cumberland Gap between Kentucky and Tennessee. **Cumberland Mountain** is in La Plata County (12,388 ft.). The name originally referred to a county in England.

Cumbres [kum′ bərz], on Colorado 17 in Conejos County, means "peaks" in Spanish. Nearby is **Cumbres Pass** (10,022 ft.). A pronunciation closer to that of Spanish would be [kōom′ brās].

Cumulus [kyoo´ myə ləs], **Mount,** on the Continental Divide between Jackson and Grand counties (12,725 ft.). Named for a type of cloud formation with rounded, mountainous outlines, but a flat base.

Curecanti [koo ri kan´ tē] **Pass,** also spelled Currecanti or Curricanti, in Gunnison County (10,450 ft.). Nearby is the geological formation called **Curecanti Needle** (7,856 ft.). Said to be named for Curicata, a Tabeguache Ute Indian chief who hunted in the area.

Custer County (est. 1877, area 737 sq. mi., pop. 1,926). The county seat is Westcliffe. Named in honor of General George A. Custer—who was killed by Indians on the Little Bighorn River in Montana in June, 1876. Formed from a section of Fremont County.

Dacono [dā kō´ nō], city on Colorado 52 in Weld County (est. 1906, inc. 1908, pop. 2,228). First established as a coal mine by C. L. Baum. As production increased, a settlement grew around the mine which Baum named Dacono, coined from the first two letters of his wife's name, Daisy, and the corresponding letters of the names of two of her friends, Cora Van Voorhies and Nona Brooks.

Dailey, on U.S. 6 in Logan County (est. 1914). When the Burlington Railroad put up a siding at this location, it named it after James Dailey, trainmaster, who came from Lincoln, Nebraska.

Dallas Divide, between Ouray and San Miguel counties (8,970 ft.), was named for George Mifflin Dallas, who was U.S. Vice President in 1845 to 1849, and whose name is also borne by Dallas, Texas. It follows the route laid out by road builder and railroad builder Otto Mears in the 1880s.

Damifino [dam i fī´ nō] **Park,** in Jackson County. Supposedly the answer to a question: "What's the name of this place?"—"Damn' if I know."

Dark Mountain, in Rocky Mountain National Park, Larimer County (10,859 ft.). Named in 1942 because the mountain is covered with dark conifers, and is near Black Canyon.

Deadman is a term occurring in many Colorado place names; there are six streams called **Deadman Creek,** and fourteen called **Deadman Gulch,** as well as a **Deadman Butte** in Larimer County (6,084 ft.). In some cases the term probably referred originally not to a corpse, but to a "deadman," pronounced [ded´ mən], meaning a log or other mass which serves as an anchor for a guy line, and is used to raise or lower loaded wagons.

De Anza [dē an´ zə] **Peak,** in Saguache County (13,333 ft.). Named for Juan Bautista de Anza (1735–88), the Spanish explorer who in 1777 to 1788 was Governor of the Spanish province of New Mexico, and explored part of what is now Colorado. Earlier, in 1776, he founded San Francisco, California.

De Beque [dē bek´], town on the Colorado River in Mesa County (est. 1889, inc. 1890, pop. 257). Named for Dr. Wallace A. E. de Beque, who settled in the locality in 1883, coming from Fairplay, Colorado. The post office was named De Beque in 1888.

Deckers, on the South Platte River and Colorado 67, in Douglas County (est. 1885?). Formerly known as Daffodil, and later as Pemberton. The name was changed in 1912 to Deckers. In earlier days, Steve Decker had a general store and saloon here.

Deep Creek. There are thirteen streams of this name in Colorado. **Deepcreek,** written as a single word, is a locale in Routt County.

Deer, either the mule deer or the black-tailed deer (two varieties of *Odocoileus hemionus*), provide names for many places in Colorado. **Deer Creek** is the name of nineteen streams, and five peaks are named **Deer Mountain;** the highest is in Lake County (13,761 ft.). **Deer Trail,** a town in Arapahoe County (est. 1870, inc. 1920, pop. 476), was founded and named by frontiersman Oliver P. Wiggins, for the place where deer drank from Bijou Creek.

Delagua [del ä´ wə] **Arroyo,** a stream in Las Animas County, is from Spanish *del agua* "of the water."

Delcarbon [del kär´ bən], on Colorado 69 in Huerfano County, is perhaps from Spanish *del carbón* "of the coal."

Delhi [del´ hī], post office on U.S. 350 in Las Animas County (est. 1899?); also pronounced [del´ ē]. Possibly named for the city in India, which was often applied to U.S. communities for its exotic quality. Once called Edwest for a resident of that name.

Del Norte [del nōrt´], town on U.S. 160, seat of Rio Grande County (est. 1872, inc. 1885, pop. 1,674); also pronounced [del nōr´ tē]. The name is from Spanish *Río Grande del Norte* "great river of the north," the name of the present Rio Grande that flows through the town.

Delta, city on U.S. 50, on the Uncompahgre River where it enters the Gunnison River (est. 1882, inc. 1882, pop. 20,980). Named for the shape of the river confluence. Formerly known as Uncompahgre, after the nearby river, mountain range, and plateau. Seat of **Delta County** (est. 1883, area 1,154 sq. mi., pop. 15,286), named after the city and created from a portion of Gunnison County.

Democrat, Mount, in Lake and Park counties (14,148 ft.). Originally known as Mount Buckskin, after a town near its base named for Joseph (Buckskin Joe) Higginbottom. Supposedly some Southerners later named the peak for their political party. It became Mount Democrat on maps after the Land Office Survey in 1883.

Denver, city on U.S. 6, 40, and 87 (est. 1858, inc. 1861, pop. 467,610). State capital of Colorado. The area's first settlement followed the discovery of placer gold at Auraria, on the west side of Cherry Creek. Another party, headed by General William Larimer of Leavenworth, Kansas, settled on the opposite side of the stream and formed the Denver City Company, named for James W. Denver, Governor of Kansas Territory. Rivalry between the two towns continued until April, 1860, when they consolidated into the municipality of Denver. There are ten other towns named Denver in the U.S. Until 1902, the city of Denver was the seat of Arapahoe County; but in that year it became a separate **Denver County** (area 95 sq. mi.), the only city-county in the state. It has the largest population and the smallest area of the sixty-three counties.

Deora [dē ōr´ ə], in Baca County (est. 1920), from Spanish *de oro* "of gold." Suggested by Postmistress Ethel Falk when the post office was established.

Derby, in Adams County (pop. 6,043), was probably named for Derby, England. **Derby Junction** and **Derby Mesa** are in Eagle County. **Derby Peak** is in Garfield County (12,186 ft.).

Desolation Peaks, in Rocky Mountain National Park, Larimer County (12,949 ft.), was named by mountain climbers; the label was made official in 1961.

Devil. Many parts of Colorado's topography have been assigned to the Devil. Many of them are straightforwardly labeled as natural features; thus there are two streams called **Devil's Creek,** four called **Devil's Gulch** or **Devil Gulch,** nine places called **Devil's Canyon,** a **Devil's Causeway,** a **Devil's Gap,** seven features called **Devil's Hole,** a **Devil's Lake,** a **Devil Mountain** (in Archuleta County, 9,992 ft.), a **Devil's Rock-pile,** and three places called **Devil's Slide.** But many places have also been described as part of the Devil's household furnishings, such as **Devil's Chair, Devil's Kitchen, Devil's Punchbowl,** and **Devil's Rocking Chair.** Finally, some places are named after the Devil's body parts: **Devil's Backbone, Devil's Elbow, Devil's Head, Devil's Nose,** and **Devil's Thumb** (the last a prominent rock formation near Boulder).

Devine [di vīn´], on U.S. 50 in Pueblo County (est. 1876?). A local tradition is that the name honors Thomas Devine, assistant secretary of the Missouri Pacific Railway in 1902; however, Missouri Pacific records do not show this. The site was first called Vineland, but was changed because of confusion with another Vineland in Pueblo County.

Dickinson, Mount, in Rocky Mountain National Park, Larimer County (11,831 ft.). Named around 1914 after Anna Dickinson, the first woman to climb Longs Peak.

Dillon, town on U.S. 6 in Summit County (est. 1880, inc. 1883, pop. 182). Named for gold seeker Tom Dillon, who became lost in the mountains; when he emerged at Golden, he described a wide valley where three rivers met. Later explorers found the area and named it in his honor. In 1961, the town was moved in its entirety to a site one mile north of its original location, because of the creation of **Dillon Reservoir.**

Dinosaur, town on U.S. 40 in Moffat County (est. 1914, inc. 1947, pop. 324). Previously known as Artesia, for a New Mexico town of the same name and for its own artesian wells. In 1965 the name was changed when the headquarters of **Dinosaur National Monument** were established here. When the town's name was changed, so were the street names; all are now called after various dinosaurs.

Diorite [dē′ ō rīt] **Peak,** in Montezuma County (12,761 ft.). Diorite is an igneous rock consisting mainly of feldspar and hornblende.

Divide, on U.S. 24 in Teller County (est. 1877). Named for its location near the divide of the Front Range, highest point on the route of U.S. 24 between the drainage basins of Fountain Creek and the South Platte River.

Dolores [də lōr′ əs], town on Colorado 145 in Montezuma County (est. 1892, inc. 1900, pop. 866). Named for the **Dolores River,** which flows through the town. Originally the settlement was about 1.5 miles down-river, and was named Big Bend because of a curve in the river. With the coming of the Rio Grande Southern Railroad, the present townsite was established and named. The full Spanish name of the river, given by Father Escalante in 1776, was *Río de Nuestra Senora de los Dolores* "River of Our Lady of Sorrows." **Dolores County** (est. 1881, area 1,026 sq. mi., pop. 1,504) is named after the same river; the seat is Dove Creek. The county was created from a part of Ouray County.

Dominguez [dō ming′ gəz], in Delta County. A common Spanish sur-name, in this case perhaps recalling Father Atanasio Dominguez of the Escalante Expedition in 1776. **Dominguez and Escalante Ruins** is the name of a prehistoric Indian site discovered by that expedition in what is now Montezuma County, the first such ruins discovered by Europeans in Colorado.

Dorothy, Lake, in Boulder County (12,061 ft.), near Arapaho Pass. Per-haps named after Dorothy, a niece of Henry Lehman, an early settler in the area.

Dotsero [dot sē′ rō], in Eagle County (est. 1880). This place was the start-ing point of the survey for the Denver and Rio Grande rail turnoff, and supposedly showed on the plats as .0 (dot zero), which gave the name. The rail point at the other end of the line was called Orestod, which is Dot-sero spelled backward. Other sources claim that this is a Ute name, but that origin has not been confirmed by Ute consultants.

Douglas County (est. 1861, area 843 sq. mi., pop. 60,391). The county seat is Castle Rock. Named in honor of Stephen A. Douglas (1813–61), who died in the year of the organization of Colorado's first counties. **Douglas Pass,** in Garfield County (8,268 ft.), is named for a White River Ute Indian chief, called Douglas by whites; his warriors killed Nathan Meeker in 1879.

Dove Creek, town on U.S. 606 (est. 1918, inc. 1939, pop. 643); seat of Dolores County. Named for a nearby stream, which in turn was named by an early freighter for the flocks of wild doves in the vicinity.

Dowd, on U.S. routes 6 and 24, in Eagle County (est. 1907?); also called Dowds Junction. Named for Jim Dowd, who opened a sawmill four miles up Mill Creek, a tributary of Gore Creek at Vail. The Denver and Rio Grande Railroad put in a spur at the junction of Gore Creek and the Eagle River, to load lumber that Dowd hauled to that point.

Downieville, on U.S. 6 and 40 in Clear Creek County, was named for William Downey, a Civil War veteran who spent a winter there on his way to California. The town of Downieville, California, is also named for him.

Doyleville, on U.S. 50 in Gunnison County (est. 1879). Named for Henry Doyle, who established a stage line here; also called Doyllestown and Doyle. The cattle and sheep raising settlement was previously known as Crooksville, and was renamed in 1885.

Drakes, on U.S. 287 in Larimer County (est. 1902?), was named for State Senator William A. Drake, who represented the district from 1903 to 1907, and who was instrumental in establishing a post office in 1905. There is also a place called **Drake** on U.S. 34 in Larimer County.

Dry Creek is the name of twenty-seven streams in the state, reflecting the seasonal nature of many western watercourses; there are also twenty-six called **Dry Gulch.**

Duck Creek is the name of three streams in Colorado, including one in Logan County.

Dumont [dōō´ mont], on U.S. 6 and 40 in Clear Creek County (est. 1860), was named for John M. Dumont, a mine owner who undertook the revival of the town and its neighboring mines. It was first named Mill City, at the delta of Mill Creek, and was a center for ore-crushing mills. When the town was rejuvenated and postal facilities restored, the name was changed because of another camp in Colorado called Mill City.

Dunckley, in Routt County, is also spelled Dunkley; it was named in 1894 for a family of early day ranchers: Bob, Richard, Tom, George, and John Dunkley. **Dunckley Pass** is in Rio Blanco County (9,763 ft.).

Dunraven, Mount, in Rocky Mountain National Park, Larimer County (12,571 ft.). Named after Windham Thomas Wyndham-Quinn, fourth earl of Dunraven and Viscount Mount Earl and Adair (1841–1926), the Irish millionaire sportsman and absentee landlord who, in the 1870s, acquired most of the Estes Park area as his private hunting preserve.

Dunton, on the Dolores River in Dolores County (est. 1892), was named for Horatio Dunton, owner of several thermal hot springs in the vicinity.

Dupont [dōo′ pont] on U.S. 6 and 85 in Adams County (post office est. 1926). For the DuPont de Nemours family of Delaware, and the company of the same name (familiarly known as the Dupont Company). The firm had several buildings here where explosives were stored. The name is French and means literally "of the bridge."

Durango [dōo rang′ gō], city on the Animas River and U.S. 160 and 550 (est. 1880, inc. 1881, pop. 12,430); seat of La Plata County. Named by former Territorial Governor A. C. Hunt after a visit to Durango, Mexico. The term is originally a Spanish family name of Basque origin.

Eads [ēdz], town on U.S. 287 (est. 1887, inc. 1916, pop. 780); seat of Kiowa County. Named for James B. Eads, a noted engineer who built the Eads Bridge across the Mississippi River at St. Louis. The settlement was originally founded with the name of Dayton when the Missouri Pacific Railroad was extended into the area, about three miles south of the townsite. When the railroad failed to reach Dayton, the town was moved, buildings and all, to the present location, and was given the new name of Eads.

Eagle, town on U.S. 6 (est. 1887, inc. 1905, pop. 1580); seat of Eagle County. First called Castle, for nearby Castle Mountain. Later the Denver and Rio Grande Western Railroad changed it to Rio Aguila, Spanish for "Eagle River." Next it was called McDonald, for the man who owned the townsite. Finally the citizens changed the name to Eagle, after the nearby **Eagle River,** which was itself named either for the golden eagle, *Aquila chrysaëtos,* or the bald eagle, *Haliaeetos leucocephalus*; both are native to Colorado. Previously **Eagle County** (est. 1883, area 1,682 sq. mi., pop. 21,928) had also been named after the river; it was created from a portion of Summit County. **Eagles Nest** is a peak in Summit County (13,420 ft.).

East Portal, in Gilpin County (est. 1925), was founded during construction of the 6.4-mile Moffat Tunnel through a shoulder of James Peak. It is named for its location at the eastern entrance of the tunnel.

Eaton, town on U.S. 85 in Weld County (est. 1888, inc. 1892, pop. 1,959). Named for Benjamin H. Eaton, fourth governor of Colorado (1885–87), a prominent builder of irrigation projects and founder of the town. First called Eatonton, to avoid conflict with Easton in El Paso County.

Echo Canyon. There are seven canyons so named in the state. **Echo Lake,** a reservoir in Clear Creek County (est. 1921), is part of Denver's Mountain Parks System.

Eckert, on Colorado 65 in Delta County, was the maiden name of Mrs. Adelbert Slates, whose husband established the first store and post office there in 1891.

Eckley, town in Yuma County (est. 1889, inc. 1920, pop. 211). An adaptation of the name of Adam Eckles, at one time cattle foreman for a well-known northeastern Colorado cattleman, J. W. Bowles.

Edgewater, city on Colorado 95, on the shore of Sloan's Lake in Jefferson County (est. 1890, inc. 1904, pop. 4,613).

Edwards, on U.S. 6 in Eagle County (est. 1882). Named for Melvin Edwards after he became Colorado Secretary of State in 1883. First known as Berry's Ranch, for Harrison Berry, owner of the townsite land. **Mount Edwards** is in Clear Creek County (13,850 ft.).

Egeria [ē jē′ rē ə], in Routt County, is named after a nymph in Roman mythology.

Egnar [eg′ nər], on Colorado 141 in San Miguel County (post office est. 1917). Reverse spelling of "range," adopted after the range land was thrown open to homesteading and a post office was established.

Eisenhower Tunnel, through the Continental Divide between Clear Creek and Summit counties (8,941 feet long), was opened in 1973. Named after U.S. President Dwight D. Eisenhower (1890–1969).

Elba, in Washington County, may have been named for the island in the Mediterranean Sea, to which Napoleon was exiled in 1814.

Elbert, in Elbert County (est. 1882). A post office at nearby Gomers Mills, opened in 1870, was moved and became the Elbert post office. The town's name was taken from that of **Elbert County** (est. 1874, area 1,864 sq. mi., pop. 9,646). The county seat is not Elbert, but Kiowa. Named in honor of Samuel H. Elbert, appointed by President Abraham Lincoln as secretary of Colorado Territory under Territorial Governor John Evans, whose daughter he married. In 1873 President Grant appointed Elbert as the sixth governor of Colorado Territory. He was serving as governor when Elbert County was created from a portion of Douglas County and from the short-lived Greenwood County. Subsequently, Samuel Elbert was elected to the state Supreme Court, where he served during 1877 to 1882 and 1886 to 1888. **Mount Elbert,** in Lake County (14,433 ft.), is also named after him; the mountain is Colorado's highest.

El Diente [el dē en′ tā] **Peak,** in Dolores County (14,159 ft.). Spanish for "the tooth," because of its jagged outline.

Eldora [el dōr′ ə], in Boulder County (est. 1896), was first established as a gold mining camp and called Eldorado. When application was made for a post office, there was confusion with Eldorado Springs, and the present version was adopted.

Eldorado [el də rod′ ō] **Springs,** on Colorado 170 in Boulder County (est. 1904); also pronounced [el də rad′ ō]. Spanish explorers in South America had a legend of an Indian ruler so rich that he gilded his body with gold dust every day, later washing it off in a lake. The name of this mythical potentate, *El Dorado* "The Gilded One," in time came to be applied to regions claimed to be rich in gold.

Elizabeth, on Colorado 86 in Elbert County (est. 1880, inc. 1890, pop. 493), was named by Governor John Evans for his sister-in-law, Elizabeth Gray Kimbark Hubbard. The governor was seeking names for new towns along the line of the Denver and New Orleans Railroad, of which he was promoter and principal owner. In 1885 this line was reorganized as the Denver, Texas and Gulf Railroad.

El Jebel, community on Colorado 82 in Eagle County, is Arabic for "The Mountain."

Elk, also known as wapiti (*Cervus elaphus*), give their name to many geographical features in Colorado. **Elk Creek** is the name of eighteen streams in the state. **Elkhead Creek** is in Moffat and Routt counties. **Elkhorn Creek** is the name of two streams in the state; there are also an Elkhorn Ditch and four Elkhorn Gulches. **Elk Mountain** is the name of seven peaks in Colorado; the highest is in Grand County (12,693 ft.). **Elk Mountains** and **West Elk Mountains** are the names of two ranges in Gunnison County. **Elk Springs,** on U.S. 40 in Moffat County (est. 1884), was named by the photographer A. G. Wallihan for the springs there, a watering place for large herds of elk. **Elkton** is on Colorado 67 in Teller County; another place so named is in Gunnison County. **Elktooth** is the most prominent point of Ogalalla Peak (12,848 ft.), on the Continental Divide between Boulder and Grand counties.

Ellicott, on Colorado 94 in El Paso County (est. 1892?), was named for the first postmaster, George Ellicott, originally from England.

El Moro [el mō´ rō], in Las Animas County (est. 1876), was originally a spur of the Denver and Rio Grande Railway. Spanish *el moro* means "the Moor" (i.e., a native of Morocco); but in New Mexico the term also refers to a horse having a bluish white color with dark brown spots. It is also possible that the place name is a misspelling of Spanish *el morro,* referring to a headland or bluff; "El Morro" exists as a place name in New Mexico.

El Paso [el pas´ ō] **County** (est. 1861, area 2,157 sq. mi., pop. 397,014). The seat is Colorado Springs, to which the name El Paso was once given. The term is Spanish for "The Pass," referring to Ute Pass, west of the settlement. One of the original seventeen territorial counties.

El Rancho [el ran´ chō], in Jefferson County (est. 1953). Established as a restaurant with the same name (Spanish for "The Ranch") by Ray Zipprich.

El Vado [el vä´ dō], on Colorado 119 in Boulder County, is Spanish for "The Ford."

Emerald Lake is the name of six bodies of water in Colorado. The name refers to the color, not to the gem stone.

Empire, town on U.S. 40 in Clear Creek County (est. 1860, inc. 1882, pop. 401). Named from the nickname of New York state, home of the four men who founded the town. First called Valley City, and later Empire City.

Enentah [ə nen´ tä], **Mount,** in Rocky Mountain National Park, Grand County (10,781 ft.). Supposedly from Arapaho *enetah-notaiyah* "man-mountain," because near its summit a fringe of pine trees made it look like a man's head. The Colorado Geographic Board decided on the spelling Enetah, but a second "n" slipped in.

Englewood, city on U.S. 285 in Arapahoe County (est. 1875, inc. 1903, pop. 29,387). Originally a pleasure resort owned by A. C. Fisk, and known as Fisk's Gardens. Later known as Orchard Place, for a large apple orchard. When the town was incorporated, residents adopted the name of Englewood, apparently for an Illinois town near Chicago. "Engle" is a variant of "Ingle," meaning a nook or corner.

Eolus [ē′ ō ləs], **Mount,** in La Plata County (14,083 ft.). First mentioned in the Hayden Survey of 1874 as Mount Aeolus, after the Greek god of the winds. The present spelling, Eolus, was used by the Wheeler Survey in 1878.

Epaulet [ep′ ə let] **Mountain,** in Clear Creek County (13,523 ft.), was so named because its shape was seen as resembling a shoulder ornament.

Erie, town in Weld and Boulder counties (est. 1871, inc. 1885, pop. 1,258). Founded as a coal-mining camp, it was supposedly named after Erie, Pennsylvania, where originally it was the name of an Indian tribe.

Escalante [es kə län′ tā], a locality on the Gunnison River in Delta County. Named for Father Francisco Silvestre Vélez Escalante, who explored southern Colorado in 1776. The name also occurs in **Escalante Forks,** a locality in Mesa County, and in **Escalante Creek,** a tributary of the Gunnison River.

Espinosa [es pi nō′ sə], on the Conejos River in Conejos County. A common Spanish family name, literally meaning "thorny."

Estabrook, in Park County, was named (with a change of spelling) for George Estabrooke, an early resident.

Estes [es′ tiz] **Park,** town on U.S. 34 in Larimer County, adjacent to Rocky Mountain National Park (est. 1905, inc. 1917, pop. 3,184); earlier known as Estes Park Village. The valley was named for the first permanent settler, Joel Estes, who came here in 1859 and built a cabin on Fish Creek. It should be noted that, in Colorado, the word "park" means not only an area for public recreation, but also a high valley surrounded by mountains; the latter meaning is the one represented in "Estes Park," as contrasted with the meaning in "Rocky Mountain National Park." Also in the area are **Estes Cone** (11,006 ft.) and **Estes Lake.**

Estrella [ə strel′ ə], on U.S. 285 in Alamosa County, is Spanish for "star." A pronunciation closer to Spanish would be [es trā′ yä].

Eureka [yōō rē′ kə], a settlement (est. 1872) in San Juan County, is from Ancient Greek, meaning "I have found it." This was a popular U.S. place name in the period of mining exploration; it was also adopted as the motto of the state of California.

Evans, city on U.S. 85 in Weld County (est. 1869, inc. 1885, pop. 5,877). Laid out by the Denver Pacific Railroad and named for the second Colorado Territorial Governor, John Evans, who served during 1862 to 1865. Evans was a leader in the financing and construction of the railroad. Earlier he was a founder of Northwestern University at Evanston, Illinois, which is also named for him. In 1864 he was a founder of the University of Denver. **Mount Evans,** a peak in Clear Creek County (14,260 ft.), is also named after him. The mountain was first named Mount Rosalie by the painter Albert Bierstadt in 1863, after his wife; but it was renamed Mount Evans in 1870. The road to its top is said to be the highest in the world.

Evergreen, on Colorado 74 in Jefferson County (est. 1866?, pop. 7,582). First called The Post, after Amos F. Post, son-in-law of Thomas Bergen, first settler of nearby Bergen Park in 1859. In 1875, D. P. Wilmot arrived in the area and acquired much of the land which is now Evergreen. Impressed with the huge trees in the area, he bestowed the name now used.

Fairchild **Mountain,** in Rocky Mountain National Park, Larimer County (13,502 ft.). Named for Lucius Fairchild of Wisconsin—who, in his capacity as commander in chief of the Grand Army of the Republic, visited Colorado in 1886.

Fairplay, town on U.S. 285 (est. 1859, inc. 1872, pop. 387); seat of Park County. Founded by gold seekers who were angered to find the best placers already taken at nearby Tarryall diggings. They found other rich deposits and established their own camp, called Fair Play as a jeer at their rivals' camp which they nicknamed "Graball."

Falcon [fal′ kən], on U.S. 24 in El Paso County (est. 1887). Named for the prairie falcon, *Falco mexicanus,* a type of hawk native to the area. The bird has been the mascot for the cadets of the United States Air Force Academy since 1955.

Falfa [fal′ fə], on Colorado 172 in La Plata County. Originally called Alfalfa for the abundance of that crop. In 1904, when the post office was established, it was changed to Falfa, since there was then another Alfalfa in Larimer County.

Fall Creek, referring to the presence of waterfalls, is the name of thirteen streams in Colorado. One, in Rocky Mountain National Park, Larimer County, is a tributary of the Cache la Poudre River; it drops about four thousand feet in a continuous succession of falls. Nearby **Fall Mountain** (12,258 ft.) is probably named after the creek. Also in the national park is **Fall River,** which was apparently named separately from the creek and the mountain. However, its water, like that of Fall Creek, eventually goes to the South Platte River. Its name gives rise to that of **Fall River Pass** (11,796 ft.).

Farisita [fâr ə sē′ tə], on Colorado 69 in Huerfano County (est. about 1855). Referred to as Huerfano Canyon as early as 1850, by settlers and travelers who used the Taos Trail over Sangre de Cristo Pass. Later known as Talpa, but changed because of the same name in New Mexico. Postmaster Asperidon S. Faris suggested the nickname of his little daughter, Jeanette, with the Spanish diminutive suffix -*ita.* The post office made the name change in 1923.

Federal Heights, city in Adams County (est. 1940, inc. 1940, pop. 9,342). Named for its location on Federal Boulevard (U.S. 287), north of Denver.

Finch Lake, in Rocky Mountain National Park, Larimer County (9,912 ft.). Named for Cassin's finch (*Carpodacus cassinii*), a bird that lives in the area.

Firestone, town in Cheyenne County (est. 1907, inc. 1908, pop. 1,358). Founded by the Denslow Coal & Land Company and named for Jacob Firestone, owner of the townsite land. The coal-mining towns of Firestone, Dacono, and Frederick have been called the "tri-cities" because of their proximity.

First View, on U.S. 40 in Cheyenne County (est. 1870). When the Kansas Pacific Railroad entered Colorado, this was the point where travelers from the east got their first glimpse of Pikes Peak and the Front Range of the Rockies.

Fitzsimons Army Hospital, in Adams County, was named in 1920 for Lieutenant William T. Fitzsimons, the first American officer killed in World War I.

Flagler, town on U.S. 24 in Kit Carson County (est. 1887, inc. 1916, pop. 564). Named for Henry M. Flagler, millionaire railroad man and associate of John D. Rockefeller. Flagler extended the Rock Island Railroad through this area. Originally the name was Malowe, for M. A. Lowe, attorney for the Rock Island. Prior to the platting of the site, there had been a combined store and post office managed by a man named Robinson, who called his post office Bowser, in memory of a favorite dog that had died.

Flatiron Mountain, in Rocky Mountain National Park, Larimer County (12,335 ft.). Named by Frank R. Koenig because of its shape. There are two other peaks so named in the state. The **Flatirons** is the name of a rock formation in Boulder County.

Flat Top is the name of six mountains in Colorado; the highest is in Gunnison County (10,572 ft.). There are also three called **Flat Top Mountain;** the highest is in Garfield County (12,354 ft.). There is a **Flat Top Peak** in San Miguel County (12,354 ft.). **Flattop Mountain,** written as a single word, is in Rocky Mountain National Park, Grand County (12,324 ft.). It gives its name to the **Flattop Peneplain,** a vast geological feature of the northern Colorado Rockies. Finally, the **Flat Tops** is an area in Garfield County.

Fleming, town on U.S. 6 in Logan County (est. 1889, inc. 1917, pop. 344). Originally a siding on the Chicago, Burlington and Quincy Railroad, and known as Twenty-Nine Mile Siding. The present site, half a mile from the original siding, was laid out in 1889 by H. B. Fleming, a representative of the Lincoln Land Company, and was named for him.

Florence, city on Colorado 67 in Fremont County (est. 1872, inc. 1887, pop. 2,990). Founded in 1860, the town was known as Frazerville, for "Uncle Joe" Frazer who developed coal mines on nearby Coal Creek. Later the name was changed to Florence, to honor the daughter of James A. McCandless; he was the first to refine oil here, in 1862, and in 1872 gave the community its first real impetus to growth by donating a townsite and having the first town plat made.

Floresta, in Gunnison County, is Spanish for "forest, thicket."

Florida [flə rē′ də] **River,** in La Plata County. Spanish for "flowering, blooming," as named by Padre Escalante in 1776. The same Spanish name, as applied to the state of Florida, has undergone a shift of accent in English.

Florissant [flōr′ i sənt], on U.S. 24 in Teller County (est. 1870). Named by Judge James Costello, the first settler, for his home town, Florissant, Missouri. The name is French for "flourishing"; however, it may have been an error for *fleurissant* "flowering." The region, once the bed of an ancient lake, is noted for its fossil remains.

Fondis [fon′ dis], in Elbert County, takes its name from an Italian hotel, the Fondi d'Italia. When a post office was established, the name was suggested by Mrs. W. S. Burns, wife of the first postmaster.

Forder, in Lincoln County, was named for Adolf Forder, an early settler.

Forks, The, in Larimer County (est. 1875). Named for its location on U.S. 287, where the road forks toward Livermore. Started by Robert O. Roberts as a hotel for lumberjacks working in the area, it was also a stage-stop on the Denver-Laramie route.

Fort Carson, in El Paso County, was named for Christopher ("Kit") Carson (1809–68), a famous frontiersman. Originally called Camp Carson. It should be noted that, in many Colorado place names, the term "fort" was applied to a civilian settlement fortified against Indian raids, not to a military reservation.

Fort Collins, city on U.S. 287 (est. 1872, inc. 1883, pop. 87,758); seat of Larimer County. Although organized as a town in 1872, it began as an army camp in 1864 with two companies of the eleventh Ohio Volunteer Cavalry from Fort Laramie, Wyoming. The site was called Camp Collins in honor of Colonel William O. Collins, commander at Fort Laramie. Later the post was renamed Fort Collins.

Fort Garland, on U.S. route 160 in Costilla County (est. 1858), was named for John Garland, commander of the military district at the time the post was founded in 1858. Kit Carson was a commander here from 1866 to 1867. The post was abandoned in 1883, but the name was retained by the settlement.

Fort Lewis, in La Plata County (est. 1877), was first established at the present site of Pagosa Springs, and was named for Lieutenant Col.

William H. Lewis. In 1880 the post was moved about twelve miles southwest of present Durango, but was abandoned a few years later. **Fort Lewis College** is now in Durango.

Fort Logan, in Arapahoe County. Named for Major Gen. John Alexander Logan, a hero of the Civil War, in his latter years a resident of Colorado.

Fort Lupton, city on U.S. 85 in Weld County (est. 1882, inc. 1890, pop. 5,159). Founded by Lancaster P. Lupton, a lieutenant in the expedition of Colonel Henry Dodge to the Rocky Mountains in 1835. Lupton took leave from the army and established a trading post around 1836, first calling it Fort Lancaster. The post was abandoned in the early 1840s, but later the adobe building was used as a stage station on the mail and express route from Missouri to Denver.

Fort Lyon, on U.S. 50 in Bent County (est. 1860?). In 1853 Colonel William Bent abandoned Bent's Fort, his famous trading post on the Arkansas River; he moved downstream about forty miles, and established a second post called Bent's New Fort. It was leased to the army, and renamed Fort Fauntleroy for a colonel of the First Dragoons. In 1859 the government purchased the site and renamed it Fort Wise, for Henry Wise, Governor of Virginia. Later it was again renamed in honor of General Nathaniel Lyon. In 1866 the river cut away the bank, and a new Fort Lyon was built about twenty miles upriver. Kit Carson died there on May 23, 1868.

Fort Morgan, city on the South Platte River and on U.S. routes 6 and 34 (est. 1884, inc. 1887, pop. 9,068); seat of Morgan County. Named for Colonel Christopher A. Morgan of the U.S. Volunteers. The former military post was first known as Camp Tyler, but in 1865 was renamed Fort Wardwell. The following year substantial buildings were erected, and the name was changed again to its present one.

Fort Vasquez [vas´ kəz], historical site in Weld County. An adobe fur trading post was built by Louis Vasquez in 1835, and was reconstructed in the 1930s.

Fosston, in Weld County (est. 1909), was platted by H. W. Foss, a British settler who gave the community his own name.

Fountain, city on U.S. 85 and 87 in El Paso County (est. 1870, inc. 1903, pop. 9,984). Named for **Fountain Creek,** which flows through the town. Early French explorers called it *La Fontaine qui Bouille* "the spring that boils," because of the bubbling springs at its head. In 1888 the town was almost totally destroyed by the explosion of a carload of blasting powder on the Denver and Rio Grande Railroad track. The complete settlement of claims against the railroad enabled the town to rebuild itself. **Fountain Valley** is also in El Paso County.

Four Corners is the area where four states, Colorado, New Mexico, Arizona, and Utah meet—the only place in the United States where this occurs.

Fourmile Creek, in Mineral and Archuleta counties, was probably so named because it is four miles from Pagosa Springs.

Fowler, town on U.S. 50 in Otero County (est. 1887, inc. 1900, pop. 1,154), was named for Professor O. S. Fowler, a phrenologist, when the town was platted in 1887. It was earlier known as South Side, then Oxford Siding, then Sibley.

Fox, in Colorado, generally refers to the red fox (*Vulpes vulpes*). **Fox Creek,** a locale on Colorado 17 in Conejos County, is named for a local stream. There are five streams so named in the state.

Foxton, in Jefferson County (est. 1876), was first named Park Siding by Dr. Alvin Morey, the founder, because of its park-like appearance. In 1909 the name was changed by J. O. Roach, a merchant, to Foxton. Supposedly the name was derived from Foxhall, a place in England.

Francisco Plaza, historical site in Huerfano County, where Colonel John M. Francisco settled in 1834. The town was subsequently named La Veta.

Franktown, on Colorado 83 and 86 in Douglas County (est. 1861?), was first known as California Ranch. Later it was named Frankstown, honoring James Frank Gardner, who owned the site. Postal authorities later deleted the "s." When Douglas County was created in 1861, Franktown was made the county seat, but lost the honor to Castle Rock in 1875. The original site is about five miles distant from the present town.

Fraser [frā′ zər], town on U.S. 40 in Grand County (est. 1871, inc. 1953, pop. 575); also pronounced [frā′ zhər]. Formerly known as Easton, for George Easton, who laid out the townsite. Its present name is derived from that of the **Fraser River** which flows through the town. The spelling was originally Frazier—for Reuben Frazier, an early settler—but postal authorities adopted the simpler spelling when the post office was established.

Frederick, town in Weld County (est. 1907, inc. 1908, pop. 988). Named for Frederick A. Clark, owner of the townsite land. Founded by three women, Mary M. Clark, Maud Clark Reynolds, and Mary Clark Steele. With Firestone and Dacono, it is one of the "tri-cities."

Fremont County (est. 1861, area 1,561 sq. mi., pop. 32,273), was named for General John C. Fremont (1813–90), famous western explorer. One of the original seventeen territorial counties, it has Canon City as its seat. **Fremont Pass,** on the Continental Divide between Lake and Summit counties (11,318 ft.), is also named for the explorer.

French Creek is the name of six streams in the state. The name may derive either from someone's surname, or from the presence of early French trappers and traders. There is also a **French Pass** in Summit County (12,046 ft.), and a **Frenchman Creek** in in Phillips County.

Frisco, town on Colorado 9 in Summit County (est. 1879, inc. 1880, pop. 1,601). For San Francisco, California. The first settler was H. A. Recen, who arrived in 1873, from Sweden.

Front Range, the range of lower mountains which extends from north to south in Colorado, east of the Continental Divide. So called because, to travelers approaching from the east, it represents the "front" of the Rockies proper.

Fruita [froo´ tə], city on U.S. 6 in Mesa County (est. 1884, inc. 1894, pop. 4,045). The site was selected in 1883 by William E. Pabor, who did much to advertise the fruit-growing area in western Colorado. Earlier called Fruitdale.

Fruitvale, community on U.S. 6 in Mesa County (pop. 5,222). Named for the orchards of the region.

Fryingpan River, a tributary of the Roaring Fork River, in Eagle and Pitkin counties. There is a story that some trappers were attacked by the Utes, and all but two were killed. One went for help—leaving the other, who was seriously wounded, in a cave. He marked the spot with a frying pan in the forks of a tree. When he returned with soldiers, the wounded one was dead, but the frying pan helped them to locate the body.

Galatea [gal ə tē′ ə], on Colorado 96 in Kiowa County (est. 1887). In Greek mythology, the name of the maiden who was carved as a statue by Pygmalion, and subsequently brought to life. Also the heroine of the novel *La Galatea,* by Miguel Cervantes, the author of *Don Quixote.*

Galena [gə lē′ nə] **Mountain.** Three peaks in Colorado are so named; the highest is in San Juan County (13,278 ft.). Galena is the principal ore of lead, consisting of crystals of lead sulfide; it is also the name of towns in Illinois, Missouri, and Kansas.

Galeton, in Weld County (est. 1909), was earlier called Zita. When the Union Pacific Railroad constructed a branch here, it chose Gale as the name for the station, probably honoring a railroad official. Confusion with the nearby town of Gill brought the change to Galeton.

Gallinas [gə yē′ nəs] **Canyon,** in Las Animas County, is from the Spanish for "'hens,'" here perhaps referring to wild turkeys.

Garcia [gär sē′ ə], in Costilla County (est. 1849); an older Anglo pronunciation is [gär′ shə]. First called Manzanares, but many early settlers belonged to interrelated families named García. The town was once part of Costilla, New Mexico, just across the state line.

Garden City, town on U.S. 85 in Weld County (est. 1935, inc. 1936, pop. 199). The name was probably suggested by the nickname of nearby Greeley, "Garden City of the West." Supposedly incorporated as a separate town because the laws of Greeley prohibited sale of intoxicants, the new town was intended to defeat the prohibition by providing a nearby supply.

Garden of the Gods, in El Paso County, was so named because of its spectacular geological formations.

Gardner, on Colorado 69 in Huerfano County (est. 1871?). In 1872 Herbert Gardner, son of Henry J. Gardner, former governor of Massachusetts, started ranching in the Huerfano Valley. The town was named for the Gardner family. Postal records show that the post office, called Huerfano Canyon before 1871, was changed that year to Gardner.

Garfield, on U.S. 50 in Chaffee County (est. 1880). Originally named Junction City, the town was renamed by postal authorities to avoid confusion with another Junction City. The present name honors President James A. Garfield (1831–81), who also gave his name to **Garfield County**

(est. 1883, area 2,996 sq. mi., pop. 29,974). The county seat is Glenwood Springs. The county was created from a portion of Summit County. There are three peaks called **Mount Garfield** in Colorado, the highest of which is in San Juan County (13,074 ft.).

Garo [gā´ rō], on Colorado 9 in Park County (est. 1863); also pronounced [gä´ rō]. A corruption of the surname of founder Adolph Guiraud, one of the first sheepmen in the state. Guiraud, born in France, came to Colorado in the early 1860s.

Gateview, on Colorado 149 in Gunnison County. Named for its view of the "Gate," a place where the Lake Fork River has cut across layers of earth and stone.

Gateway, on Colorado 141 in Mesa County (est. 1890, pop. 7,510). Selected because of its location at the "gateway" of the old Ute Trail into the mountainous country to the southwest and northeast.

Gemini [jem´ i nī] **Peak,** in Park County (13,951 ft.). The name is Latin for "twins"; it refers to a constellation and a sign of the zodiac.

Gem Village, on U.S. 160 in La Plata County (est. 1942). Founded by Frank Morse, who was in the gem and mineral business in Bayfield. He established a colony for artists and artisans, and it became a rock hunter's haven.

Genesee [jen´ ə sē] **Park,** community on U.S. 40 in Jefferson County (pop. 2,737). Probably named after Genesee, New York. The Iroquoian name is said to mean "beautiful valley."

Genoa [jen´ ō ə], town on U.S. 24 in Lincoln County (est. 1888, inc. 1905, pop. 167). Probably named for Genoa, Italy. Earlier called Creech, for one of the contractors for the Rock Island Lines Railroad; and later Cable, for R. R. Cable, president of the Rock Island.

George, Mount, in Grand County (12,876 ft.). Perhaps named for Russell D. George, who was Colorado State Geologist from 1907 onward.

Georgetown, town on U.S. 6 (est. 1864, inc. 1885, pop. 89); seat of Clear Creek County. Gold was discovered near here by the Griffith brothers, David and George, in 1859, and two mining camps sprang up. One was Georgetown, for George Griffith, and the other Elizabethtown, for a Griffith sister. In a public meeting, the two camps were united under the present name.

Gilcrest [gil′ krest], town on U.S. 85 in Weld County (est. 1908, inc. 1912, pop. 1,084). Originally a sidetrack and sugar beet dump called Nantes. Named by W. K. Gilcrest, who bought large amounts of land here and organized a bank.

Gill [gil], on Colorado 37 in Weld County (est. 1909). Named for William H. Gill, president of the Gill-Deckers Improvement Company. The company sold seventy-three acres of land to the Union Pacific Railroad, which built a depot and named the prospective town.

Gilman [gil′ mən], on U.S. 24 in Eagle County (est. 1886). In honor of H. M. Gilman, a prominent mining man. Earlier names were Clinton, Battle Mountain, and Rock Creek.

Gilpin [gil′ pin], a locality in **Gilpin County** (est. 1861, area 148 sq. mi., pop. 3,070). The county seat is not Gilpin, but Central City. Both the settlement and the county were named in honor of Colonel William Gilpin, first governor of Colorado Territory (1861–62). It is one of the original seventeen counties, and one of the three which retains the 1861 boundaries. Next to the City and County of Denver, it is the smallest of the sixty-three counties. There is another locale called **Gilpin** in Bent County, and a **Gilpin Peak** between Ouray and San Miguel counties (13,694 ft.).

Gilsonite [gil′ sə nīt], in Mesa County. A trade name applied to uintaite, a type of natural asphalt, named for the Uintah mountains in Utah.

Glacier [glā′ shər] is a term found in many Colorado place names. There are two streams called **Glacier Creek,** and **Glacier Knobs** are a geological feature in Rocky Mountain National Park, Larimer County (10,225 ft.). **Glacier Peak** (12,853 ft.) and **Glacier Mountain** (12,443 ft.) are both in Summit County.

Glade Park, in Mesa County (est. 1910), is so named because the top of adjacent Piñon Mesa opens into a large, heavily wooded park.

Gladstone [glad′ stōn], in San Juan County (est. 1878). Named for British Prime Minister William E. Gladstone (1809–98) by a group of four admirers, three of whom were British subjects.

Glen, meaning "a small valley," is from Gaelic *gleann.* It is used in several Colorado place names, such as **Glen Comfort,** on U.S. 34 in Larimer County. **Glen Eyrie** [ē′ rē] is in El Paso County; an eyrie is an eagle's nest. **Glen Haven,** in Larimer County (est. 1903), was named by a Presbyterian missionary, William H. Schureman, for its peaceful surroundings. The Presbyterian Assembly Association purchased the land, settled by Orren S. Knapp in 1897, as a summer home resort. The community is at the foot of Devil's Gulch, a term the missionary felt was blasphemous.

Glendale, city on Colorado 2 and 83 in Arapahoe County (est. 1952, inc. 1952, pop. 2,453). Presumably named for the pleasant associations of "glen" and "dale"; towns with the same name exist in several other states. The community was incorporated to escape annexation to Denver.

Glendevey [glen dā′ vē], in Larimer County (est. 1902). Former Mississippi River skipper, Thomas ("Cap") Davy, bought a ranch in a glen, and called the post office Glen Davy. In later years the spelling was changed to Glendevey. The post office site was moved about four times before it eventually closed.

Glenwood Springs, city on U.S. 6 (est. 1882, inc. 1885, pop. 6,561); seat of Garfield County. Once called Defiance; then named Glenwood Hot Spring, after Glenwood, Iowa, and for the mineral springs in the vicinity.

Gold Creek is the name of seven streams in the state, and gold figures in many other place names. However, **Golden,** a city on U.S. 6 (est. 1859, inc. 1886, pop. 13,116), and seat of Jefferson County, was named for Thomas L. Golden—who, with James Saunders and George W. Jackson, established a temporary camp near the mouth of Clear Creek Canyon in 1858. Though they took preliminary steps toward laying out a townsite, the city was actually established by the Boston Company, headed by George West. From 1862 to 1867 it was the capital of Colorado Territory.

Gold Hill, in Boulder County, was named during the gold rush of the 1850s. A sign at the edge of town reads as follows:

GOLD HILL
Est. — 1,859
Elev. — 8,463
Pop. —   118
Total   10,440

Goliath Peak, in Clear Creek County (12,216 ft.), was named for the biblical giant defeated by David.

Goodale, in Prowers County, was named for a Lamar attorney, C. G. Goodale.

Goodrich, on Colorado 39 and 144 in Morgan County (est. 1882). Named for Gus T. Goodrich, a Morgan County pioneer and member of the first Board of County Commissioners.

Gore Pass, in Grand County (9,527 ft.). Named for the sportsman Sir St. George Gore, who came from England to explore the area, bringing with him fifty servants, thirty supply wagons, and packs of hunting dogs. **Gore Mountain** is in Routt County (10,687 ft.); the **Gore Range** is in Grand County, Eagle County, and Summit County.

Gotera [gō târ ə] **Canyon,** in Las Animas County. The Spanish word means "leak, gutter."

Gothic, in Gunnison County (est. 1879.). Named for nearby **Gothic Mountain** (12,625 ft.), so called from rock formations suggestive of medieval architecture.

Gould [gōōld], on Colorado 14 in Jackson County (est. 1936), was named for Edward B. Gould, who settled a homestead in 1898. An earlier informal community in the area was called Penfold. The community of Gould started with the sale of a large timber tract in North Park.

Gowanda, on Colorado 66 in Weld County, is probably named after Gowanda, New York. Said to be a shortening of an Iroquois expression meaning "almost surrounded by hills."

Granada [grə nä′ də], town on U.S. 50 and 385 in Prowers County (est. 1873, inc. 1887, pop. 513); also pronounced [grə nā′ də]. Originally at the mouth of Granada Creek, probably named for the city and former kingdom of Spain, popularized in Washington Irving's *Conquest of Granada* (1829). The town was created by the Atchison, Topeka and Santa Fe Railway when the line was extended to this point. After the railhead pushed on to La Junta in 1876, the town was moved to its present site.

Granby, town on U.S. 40 in Grand County (est. 1904, inc. 1905, pop. 966). Apparently named for Granby Hillyer, a Denver attorney. **Lake Granby** is named for the town.

Grand County (est. 1874, area 1,854 sq. mi., pop. 7,966). The county seat is Hot Sulphur Springs. Named for the Grand River, the name by which the upper part of the Colorado River was earlier known. The county was formed from a portion of Summit County. Several other Colorado place names are also derived from the name of the Grand River, including

Grand Ditch, in Grand County—a channel dug to collect water from the headwaters of the Colorado River, in the Never Summer Mountains, and carry it across the Continental Divide, at La Poudre Pass, to Long Draw Reservoir in Larimer County.

Grand Junction, city on U.S. 6 and 50 (est. 1881, inc. 1882, pop. 29,034), and seat of Mesa County, was named for its location at the junction of the Gunnison and Grand (later Colorado) rivers. Earlier known as Ute.

Grand Lake, in Grand County, is the largest natural body of water in Colorado; it gives its name to the town of **Grand Lake,** on U.S. 34 (est. 1879, inc. 1944, pop. 259), founded as a mining settlement by the Grand Lake Town & Improvement Company.

Grand Valley was once the name of the post office at Parachute, in Garfield County.

Graneros [grə när′ ōs] **Creek,** in Pueblo County, represents the plural of Spanish *granero* "granary."

Granite, on U.S. 24 in Chaffee County (est. 1860?). Probably for the barren outcroppings of rock in the vicinity. The old gold-mining camp was once the seat of Lake County, and the temporary seat of Chaffee County after it was formed.

Grant, on U.S. 285 in Park County (est. 1870), was probably named for President Ulysses S. Grant (1822–85). Once known as Grantville.

Grape Creek is the name of three streams in Colorado. The name probably refers to the wild grape, *Vitis riparia.*

Grays Peak, in Clear Creek and Summit counties (14,270 ft.). Named for a celebrated botanist, Asa Gray; the name was given in 1861 by Charles C. Parry, who also named nearby Torreys Peak. Earlier the pair was known to prospectors as the "Twin Peaks."

Great Dikes of the Spanish Peaks, in Huerfano County, refers to hundreds of intrusive igneous rock walls radiating out from a center.

Great Divide, in Moffat County (est. 1916). Believed to have been named for the *Great Divide,* a weekly publication issued by *The Denver Post* from 1914 to 1918. The community had a *Great Divide Sentinel* in 1917 to 1918. The term was formerly used for what is now called the Continental Divide.

Great Sand Dunes, a National Monument and Wilderness in Saguache and Alamosa counties.

Greeley, city on U.S. 34 and 85 (est. 1870, inc. 1885, pop. 60,536); seat of Weld County. Named for Horace Greeley of the *New York Tribune,* who was impressed with the agricultural possibilities of the country when he visited the West in 1859. When his agricultural editor, Nathan C. Meeker, made a trip west, he conceived a plan to found a colony, and Greeley began a publicity campaign in his paper. The Union Colony was organized and bought a townsite, named in Greeley's honor.

Green, as a term in place names, may refer to verdure, or in some cases may be a family name. The term is applied to many natural features in Colorado; thus there are fifteen peaks called **Green Mountain,** the highest of which is in San Juan County (13,049 ft.). One of the smaller of these peaks gives its name to the community of **Green Mountain,** in Jefferson County. **Green Mountain Falls** is a town in El Paso and Teller counties (est. 1889, inc. 1890, pop. 663); it was named for a series of cascades cutting the side of the nearby mountain.

Greenhorn, in Pueblo County, was named after **Greenhorn Mountain,** between Pueblo and Huerfano counties (12,349 ft.). The term is a translation of Spanish *Cuerno Verde,* the name of a Comanche chief killed here by Governor Juan Bautista de Anza in 1779. The name is garbled in the nearby community of Cuerna Verde Park. Elsewhere the term "greenhorn" probably refers to a newcomer in the country, as in **Greenhorn Creek,** the name of streams in Eagle and Pueblo counties.

Green River is a tributary of the Colorado River; it rises in Wyoming and enters Moffatt County, in northwestern Colorado, before continuing into Utah.

Greenwood is the name of localities both in Pueblo County and in Custer County. **Greenwood County** (est. 1870, abolished 1874), was named for Colonel W. N. Greenwood, who was in charge of constructing the Kansas Pacific Railway. It was divided into Bent and Elbert counties. **Greenwood Village** is a city on Colorado 88 in Arapahoe County (est. 1950, inc. 1950, pop. 7,509).

Greystone, in Moffat County (est. 1882?). In the Brown's Hole area, a hiding place for cattle rustlers and desperadoes. In 1921, Henry Kenealy, the first postmaster, named the place Greystone for the rocks in the vicinity.

Grizzly refers to the grizzly bear (*Ursus arctos*), now probably extinct in the state. Colorado has three streams called **Grizzly Creek,** plus seven called **Grizzly Gulch,** and four bodies of water called **Grizzly Lake.** There are five mountains called **Grizzly Peak;** the highest is in Pitkin County (13,988 ft.). There is also a **Grizzly Mountain** in Chaffee County (13,723 ft.).

Groundhog is a term for the animal otherwise known as the woodchuck or yellow-bellied marmot, *Marmota flaviventris.* **Groundhog Creek** is the name of three streams in Colorado; there are also three called **Groundhog Gulch.** A body of water in Dolores County is called **Groundhog Reservoir.** A peak called **Groundhog Mountain** is in Dolores and San Miguel counties (12,165 ft.).

Grover [grō´ vər], town in Weld County (est. 1888, inc. 1916, pop. 135). Named by Mrs. Neal Donovan, pioneer settler, who gave it her maiden name. The first post office, about a mile north of the present town, was called Catoga.

Guadalupe [gwä də lōō´ pē], in Conejos County, was named in 1854 for Our Lady of Guadalupe, the patroness of Mexico. Her shrine is on the outskirts of Mexico City. Guadalupe is also a common Spanish name given women.

Guajatoyah [wä hə toi´ yə] **Creek** (also spelled Guajatah, Guajatolla, and Guayotoyo), in Las Animas County. There is also a Wahatoya Creek, sometimes spelled Guajatoyah, in Huerfano County. The name reflects an Ute word for the Spanish Peaks, meaning simply "paired peaks."

Guanella [gwa nel´ ə] **Pass,** in Clear Creek County (11,669 ft.). Named for Byron Guanella, the county road supervisor who planned the route in the 1950s. The name is of Italian origin.

Guero [wâr´ ō], **Mount,** in Gunnison County (12,052 ft.), is said to reflect the Spanish name of a Ute Indian chief. The Spanish term (also spelled *huero*) means "fair in complexion."

Guffey, in Park County (est. 1890?). An early gold-mining camp first called Idaville, then Freshwater. It takes its name from J. K. Guffey, a pioneer settler.

Gulnare [gul´ nər], on the Apishapa River in Las Animas County (est. 1884); also pronounced [gul när´]. Once known as Abeyton, but the post office was taken from the postmaster for some irregularity. A new name was to be decided, and names were submitted to postal authorities in Washington. On the envelope in which these were mailed was the picture of a blooded Holstein cow with her name, "Princess of Gulnare." The post office discarded the submitted names and selected Gulnare.

Gunbarrel, community on Colorado 119 in Boulder County (pop. 9,388). Supposedly because the road through there is "straight as a gunbarrel."

Gunnison, city on U.S. 50 (est. 1880, inc. 1880, pop. 4,636). First known as Richardson's Colony. The city is the seat of **Gunnison County** (est. 1877, area 3,220 sq. mi., pop. 10,273), formed from part of Lake County. Both city and county are named for the **Gunnison River;** this in turn was named for Captain John W. Gunnison who led a surveying party through the area in 1853 in search of a railroad route to the west. Gunnison and most of his company were killed by Ute Indians in Utah in the fall of the same year. The Gunnison River rises in this county, and flows through Delta and Mesa counties to join the Colorado River.

Guyot [gē′ ō], **Mount,** a peak in Summit County (13,370 ft.). Named by botanist Charles C. Parry for the Swiss-born geologist Arnold Henry Guyot (1807–84), after whom are also named mountains in Tennessee and California.

Gypsum [jip′ səm], town on U.S. 6 in Eagle County (est. 1887, inc. 1911, pop. 1,750). Named for large deposits of the mineral calcium sulfate. **Gypsum Valley** (San Miguel County) is a translation of Spanish *Cañón del Yeso,* a name given by the Dominguez-Escalante expedition in 1776.

Hagerman [hā′ gər mən] **Peak,** in the Elk Mountains of Gunnison County (13,841 ft.), was named for Percy Hagerman, businessman and mountaineer, who climbed this mountain in 1907.

Hagues Peak, in Rocky Mountain National Park, Larimer County (13,560 ft.). Named for James and Arnold Hague of Boston, surveyors and geologists who worked in the area in the 1870s.

Hahns Peak, a location in Routt County (est. 1864), was named for a nearby mountain (10,389 ft.), named in turn for a German prospector called Joseph Henne, Henn, or Hahn.

Haiyaha [hä yä′ hä] **Lake,** in Rocky Mountain National Park, Larimer County. Said to be an Arapaho word for "rock."

Halandras [hə lan′ drəs] **Gulch,** in Rio Blanco County, is named after Regas K. Halandras, a native of Greece who settled in Colorado.

Hale, on the Republican River in Yuma County (est. 1887). The first store and post office was operated by Richard Taylor, a Civil War veteran, who named the place after Nathan Hale (1755–76), a patriot of the American Revolution.

Hallett Peak, on the Continental Divide in Rocky Mountain National Park, between Grand and Larimer counties (12,713 ft.). Named for rancher William L. Hallett, one of the founders of the Rocky Mountain Club and an outstanding climber.

Hamilton, on Colorado 13 in Moffat County (est. 1885), was named for Tom and Riley Hamilton, early settlers.

Handies Peak, in Hinsdale County (14,048 ft.). Named for a San Juan area man, said by some to be a surveyor, before 1874.

Hanging Flume, a historic site in Montrose County, consists of the ruins of a six-mile long wooden channel, designed to supply water for gold mining to arid Mesa Creek Flats.

Hardin, on the South Platte River in Weld County. Named for Lieutenant George H. Hardin, who was once stationed at Camp Weld, and later became a resident of the area.

Hardscrabble Creek, in Custer County. About 1845 a number of Ute Indians are said to have surprised and killed some settlers along the Huerfano River. Others escaped up a streambed; they described their flight as a "hard scramble" or "scrabble," and the creek was thus named. Nearby is **Hardscrabble Pass** (altitude 8,800 ft.).

Harris, on U.S. 40 in Routt County. Named for George W. Harris, an officer of the Colorado and Utah Coal Company.

Hartman, town on Colorado 196 in Prowers County (est. 1906, inc. 1910, pop. 108). Because of a clerical error in the Chicago offices of the Santa Fe Railway, the town was named for George Hartman, a former company superintendent. The intention had been to name it for C. H. Bristol, an assistant general manager of the road, who owned land near Hartman. At the same time another town, near which Hartman owned property, was named for Bristol. The mistake was never corrected.

Hartsel [härt′ səl], on the south fork of the South Platte River and U.S. 24, in Park County (est. 1866). For Samuel Hartsel, pioneer cattleman, who came to the region from Pennsylvania about 1860. Hartsel was unable to find gold, and began buying travel-worn oxen from wagon trains coming in from the East. He fattened, rested, and resold the animals to travelers returning eastward. Later he acquired purebred shorthorns and founded the stock-raising industry in South Park.

Harvard, Mount, in Chaffee County (14,420 ft.). Colorado's third-ranking peak, and highest of the Collegiate Group in the Sawatch Range. Named and measured in 1869 by Professor Josiah Dwight Whitney, first head of the Harvard Mining School, whose name was given to Mount Whitney in California. Whitney's survey party included several graduates of Harvard University.

Hasty, on U.S. 50 in Bent County (est. 1907). First homesteaded in 1886, it was settled in 1907 by W. A. Hasty and George Hill. A townsite was laid out and the Santa Fe Railway named the settlement for Hasty.

Haswell [haz′ wel], town on Colorado 96 in Kiowa County (est. 1905, inc. 1920, pop. 62). A number of consecutive stations on the Missouri Pacific Railroad were supposedly named by the daughter of Jay Gould, the railroad magnate. The names had their initial letters in alphabetical order as one approached Pueblo from the east. The stations so named were: Arden, Brandon, Chivington, Diston, Eads, Fergus, Galatea, Haswell, Inman, Jolliett, Kilburn, Lolita, Meredith, Nepesta, Olney, and Puetney. The reason for the choice of the name Haswell is not known. Many of the names in this group have long been out of use.

Hawley, on Colorado 10 and 71 in Otero County (est. 1908). Originally a beet dump for the American Beet Sugar Company of Rocky Ford. It was named about 1908 for Floyd Hawley, who for years was cashier of the sugar firm.

Haxtun, town on U.S. 6 in Phillips County (est. 1888, inc. 1909, pop. 952). Established when the Burlington Railroad built a line here in 1888. The name honors one of the railroad contractors. Spelling variants are Haxtum and Haxton.

Haybro, on Colorado 131 in Routt County, was supposedly named for the Hayden Brothers, coal operators.

Hayden, town on U.S. 40 in Routt County (est. 1894, inc. 1906, pop. 1,444). The first houses here were built in 1875 by Major J. B. Thompson and Colonel P. M. Smart. They named the settlement in honor of Ferdinand V. Hayden, head of the U.S. Geological & Geographic Survey, who led a survey of Colorado starting in the late 1860s.

Haynach [hā′ nak] **Lakes,** in Rocky Mountain National Park, Grand County. From Arapaho *hííínech* "snow water."

Heartstrong, in the sand hills of Yuma County (est. 1920). Founded by Cleve Mason, who earlier (1908) founded and owned Happyville, two miles east. After selling Happyville to a cooperative, he built another store, garage, and filling station. Friction between Mason and the co-op made Mason decide to move to a new location, but his choice of name has not been explained.

Heeney, on Green Mountain Reservoir in Summit County (est. 1938). For Paul Heeney, owner of much land bordering Green Mountain Dam when it was built in 1938.

Henderson, on U.S. 85 in Adams County (est. 1859). Named for Captain (sometimes called Colonel) Jack Henderson, a freighter who reached Auraria (Denver) with a wagon train of supplies in 1858. On a parcel of land in the Platte River, he set up the first feed yard and public corral in the region. The island became known as Henderson's Island, and the community which grew up along the river bank also took Henderson's name.

Henson, in Hinsdale County, was named for Henry Henson, who prospected in the area in 1871.

Hereford [hûr′ fərd], on Colorado 14 in Weld County (est. 1902). Named for a breed of white-faced cattle, popular in the region since early days. A Hereford station was established by the Burlington Railroad in 1886, just north of the Colorado line. In 1888 a post office of the same name was created in Weld County. In 1902, Frank Benton named his ranch and small settlement in Colorado "New Hereford," but the "new" was later dropped.

Hermosa [hər mō′ sə], on U.S. 550 in La Plata County (est. 1874?). A station on the Denver and Rio Grande Western Railroad line to Silverton. The founders are said to have selected the name, which is Spanish for "beautiful," as descriptive of its location. A post office was established in 1874, but no mail was delivered until the following year, when the first mail was brought over the range from Howardsville by snowshoers. There is a **Hermosa Peak** in Dolores County (12,579 ft.).

Hesperus [hes′ pə rəs], on Colorado 140 and 160 in La Plata County (est. 1882). Settled in 1882 with the opening of the Hesperus Coal Mine by John A. Porter, it was named by the Rio Grande Southern Railroad for **Hesperus Mountain,** in Montezuma County (13,232 ft.), northwest of town. The name is Latin for the evening star, which shines in the west.

Hessie, a ghost town in Boulder County, was named by J. H. Davis for his wife.

Hiamovi [hē ə mō′ vē] **Mountain,** in Grand County. Apparently an Indian name drawn from *The Indians' Book,* by Natalie Curtis, published in 1908. According to Curtis, Hiamovi (said to mean High Chief), was a Cheyenne who helped her collect songs, legends, and pictures.

Hiawatha [hī′ ə wä′ thə], in Moffat County (est. 1926?), was named for the Algonkian Indian hero celebrated in Longfellow's poem.

Hideaway Park, in Grand County (est. 1905?), was named for its secluded location, after earlier being called Woodstock, Vasquez, and Little Chicago. Max Kortz, who owned a dance hall in the village, is believed to have applied the present name.

Hierro [hī′ rō], on the Gunnison River and U.S. 50, in Gunnison County. The word is Spanish for "iron," in the present case perhaps meaning a branding iron. A pronunciation closer to Spanish would be [yâr′ ō].

Hillrose, town in Morgan County (est. 1900, inc. 1919, pop. 169). Settled by the Lincoln Land Company, the Burlington Railroad's townsite corporation. Mrs. Kate Emerson of Denver, who had deeded land for the townsite, was permitted by the railroad to select the town's name. She reversed her sister's name, Rose Hill, to make Hillrose.

Hillside, on Colorado 69 in Fremont County (est. 1880?). Mrs. Seth Brown, postmistress in 1884, named the settlement after her family's ranch, Hillside. Previously the post office was called Texas Creek.

Hinsdale [hinz′ dāl] **County** (est. 1874, area 1,054 sq. mi., pop. 467). The county seat is Lake City. Named for George A. Hinsdale, a pioneer leader in southern Colorado. A former lieutenant governor, he died during the month preceding the creation of Hinsdale County, which was formed from portions of Conejos and Summit counties. Lake City is the only community in the county, which ranks as the state's least populous.

Hoehne [hō′ nē], on Colorado 239 in Las Animas County (est. 1886). Named for William Hoehne, a German pioneer settler who came to the region in the 1860s. Known as "Dutch Bill," Hoehne built the first mill and irrigation ditch, the beginning of extensive irrigation in the area. The Hoehne post office was moved from Pulaski, where it had opened in 1874.

Holly, town on U.S. 50 in Prowers County (est. 1896, inc. 1903, pop. 877). Named for Hiram S. Holly, pioneer rancher, who established the SS Ranch, which originally extended from Granada to the Kansas border.

Holyoke [hō′ lē ōk], city on U.S. 6 (est. 1887, inc. 1888, pop. 1,931); seat of Phillips County. Named for Holyoke, Massachusetts, which in turn was named for the Reverend Edward Holyoke, an early president of Harvard College. Phillips County was created in 1889 from the southern part of Logan County.

Home, in Larimer County. Said to have been named by John R. Brown as his "mountain home." When he applied for a post office, he was told there were too many "Mountain Homes" in the U.S., so the word Mountain was omitted.

Homelake, in Rio Grande County (est. 1890). Created as the State Soldiers and Sailors Home on land donated by the town of Monte Vista, on what was called Stanger Lake (now Homelake). The first buildings were opened and dedicated to Civil War veterans in November, 1891. In 1965, the Colorado Legislature passed an act changing the name to Colorado State Veterans Center.

Hondius [hon′ dē əs] **Park,** in Rocky Mountain National Park, Larimer County. Named for Pieter Hondius, a settler from Holland who arrived in 1896.

Hooper [ho͞op′ ər], town on Colorado 17 and 112 in Alamosa County (est. 1891, inc. 1898, pop. 112); also pronounced [ho͞o′ pər]. First called Garrison, after the mercantile firm of Garrison & Howard. Confusion resulted between the names of Gunnison and Garrison; the latter was then changed to Hooper, for Major Shadrach Hooper, passenger agent for the Denver and Rio Grande Railroad.

Hoosier [ho͞o′ zhər] **Pass,** on the Continental Divide between Park and Summit counties (11,541 ft.). Supposedly named about 1860 by gold prospectors from Indiana, the "Hoosier State." Another Hoosier Pass is in Teller County.

Horse Creek is the name of eighteen streams in Colorado; there are also eight called **Horse Gulch.** There are six peaks named **Horse Mountain;** the highest is in Mesa County (10,689 ft.).

Horseshoe Lake is the name of five bodies of water in Colorado; there are also three streams called **Horseshoe Creek.** There are three peaks called **Horseshoe Mountain;** the highest is in Lake County (13,898 ft.).

Horsetooth Peak is in Rocky Mountain National Park, Boulder County (10,344 ft.). There is also a **Horsetooth Mountain** near Fort Collins in Larimer County (7,255 ft.).

Hotchkiss, town on Colorado 92 and 133 in Delta County (est. 1881, inc. 1901, pop. 744). Named for Enos Hotchkiss, an early settler.

Hot Sulphur Springs, town on the Colorado River and U.S. 40 (est. 1860, inc. 1903, pop. 347); seat of Grand County. Named for the hot springs in the area. The townsite was once owned by William N. Byers, founder of the Denver *Rocky Mountain News.*

Hovenweep [hō′ vən wēp] **Canyon,** partly in Montezuma County; the main location is in an adjacent area of Utah. The National Monument here preserves pre-Columbian Indian ruins. From a Ute name containing *wíiyap* "canyon."

Howard, on U.S. 50 in Fremont County (est. 1880?). Named for **Howard Creek,** named in turn for John Howard, who settled here in 1876. **Howard Mountain,** on the Continental Divide between Jackson and Grand counties (12,810 ft.), is perhaps named for an early prospector in the area. **Howardsville,** in San Juan County, is named for Lieutenant George W. Howard, who accompanied the Baker Party to this location in 1869 to 1871.

Hoyt, in Morgan County (est. 1882?), was the original homestead of Mrs. Sidney Davis Hoyt. Her son, Dr. James A. Hoyt, was also a surveyor, and the town was named for him.

Hudson, town on U.S. 6 in Weld County (est. 1887, inc. 1914, pop. 918). For the Hudson City Land & Improvement Company of Denver, which purchased and developed the townsite.

Huerfano [wâr´ fə nō] **County** (est. 1861, area 1,574 sq. mi., pop. 6,009). The county seat is Walsenburg. The county, one of the seventeen original divisions of Colorado Territory, was named after the **Huerfano River,** which in turn was named from **Huerfano Butte,** an isolated, cone-shaped butte in the river bottom. The name is from Spanish *huérfano* "orphan," referring to the isolation of the butte. Old-fashioned Anglo pronunciations are [ōr´ fə nō, wûr´ fə nō].

Hugo, town on U.S. 40 and 287 (est. 1874, inc. 1909, pop. 660); seat of Lincoln County. Supposedly for a pioneer settler named Richard Hugo. Another source reports that the town was named for French novelist Victor Hugo.

Humboldt [hum´ bōlt] **Peak,** in Custer County (14,064 ft.). Part of the Crestone Group in the Sangre de Cristo Range, this peak is named for the German explorer and geographer Alexander von Humboldt (1769–1859). A German colony was started in the Wet Mountain Valley, and one of the best-producing mines the colonists discovered was named the Humboldt Mine.

Huron Peak, in Chaffee County (14,005 ft.), was a latecomer to the list of high peaks, but was resurveyed in 1956 and topped the 14,000-foot mark. It was probably named for the Huron Indians, an Iroquoian tribe of the Great Lakes area.

Husted [hyōō´ stəd], in El Paso County, was named for a rancher in the area.

Hyannis [hī an´ is] **Peak,** in Pitkin County (11,602 ft.). Probably named for Hyannis, Massachusetts, which took the name of a local Indian chief in the seventeenth century.

Hygiene, in Boulder County (est. 1861). After an early sanitarium, Hygiene Home, established by a Dunkard preacher, Jacob S. Flory. A group from Pella, Iowa, settled near the present town and called the place Pella. A post office later was moved northeast and the settlement called North Pella. The Reverend Flory built between the two Pellas, and was the first postmaster of the town which absorbed the two Pellas and became Hygiene.

Ida, **Mount,** in Rocky Mountain National Park, on the Continental Divide between Grand and Larimer counties (12,880 ft.). Perhaps named for Mount Ida near ancient Troy, mentioned in the *Iliad;* or else from a woman's name.

Idaho Springs, city on Clear Creek and on U.S. 6 and 40 (est. 1860, inc. 1885; pop. 1,834). The seat of Clear Creek County. Originated as the camp of George A. Jackson, who discovered gold in the area in 1859; the settlement has also been known as Jackson's Diggings, Sacramento City, Idaho, Idaho City, and Idahoe. The origin of the name is in *ídààhé^n*, literally "enemy," a name given by the Kiowa-Apache Indians to the Comanche tribe which they met in eastern Colorado. In the 1850s, the name was applied to the region of the present state; and in 1860 it was not only given to the settlement of Idaho Springs, but was proposed to the U.S. Congress for what they decided to call Colorado Territory. The name evidently had appeal in other parts of the west, and in 1861 a region in Washington Territory was named Idaho County. When that region was itself organized as a territory in 1863, the proposal was made that it be called Montana Territory; however, the U.S. Senate gave the name Idaho Territory to what later became the state of Idaho. (Full details are given by Erl H. Ellis in his booklet *That word "Idaho,"* published by the University of Denver in 1951.)

  In fact, this is part of an even more complex history of place name shift. The name Montana (from Spanish *montaña* "mountain") was first applied to a town near Pike's Peak, in what was then part of Kansas, but later became Colorado. The town subsequently disappeared; however, the name struck the fancy of U.S. Representative James Ashley of Ohio—

the man who proposed, in 1863, that Idaho County, in the Washington Territory, should be named Montana Territory. After that proposal failed, Ashley made another try in 1864, and this time succeeded in giving the name Montana Territory to what later became the state of Montana.

Idalia [ī dāl′ yə], in Yuma County (est. 1887). For Mrs. Edaliah Helmick, wife of one of the original settlers, with a simplification in spelling. Originally the site was about a half-mile west of the present location. It was first known as Friend, for a town in Nebraska, from which some of the region's settlers came.

Idledale, in Jefferson County (est. 1905?). Founded by John C. Starbuck, first as a guest ranch, and later a popular summerhome community. Although first named for Starbuck, it was also known as Joyland in the 1920s. In 1932 a flood in Bear Creek Canyon destroyed lives and property; in an effort to help erase the bad memories, the name was changed to Idledale. The name was meant to suggest unhurried summer living in the mountains.

Ignacio [ig nash′ ē ō], town on Colorado 172, on the Southern Ute Indian Reservation in La Plata County (est. 1910, inc. 1913, pop. 720); also pronounced [ig nä′ sē ō]. Named for Chief Ignacio, of the Weminuche Band of the Utes; the name is the Spanish equivalent of "Ignatius." It is the headquarters of the Southern Ute Indian Reservation, and the site of an Indian school and hospital. The town land was purchased from the tribe in 1910.

Iliff [ī′ lif], town on Colorado 138 in Logan County (est. 1881, inc. 1926, pop. 174). Named for John W. Iliff, an early cattle king, whose L. F. Ranch embraced the townsite. Iliff's widow gave a large part of his estate to the founding of the Iliff School of Theology.

Illinois River, in Jackson County, is a tributary of the Michigan River (which in turn flows into the North Platte River). Named for the state, which in turn is named for an Algonkian Indian tribe. The term in their own language means simply "men."

Independence, on Colorado 82 in Pitkin County, is so named because it was founded on Independence Day in 1879. It gives its name to **Independence Pass,** on the Continental Divide between Lake and Pitkin counties (12,095 ft.). There is another locale called **Independence** in Teller County and **Independence Mountain** (12,614 ft.) in Summit County.

Indian, as an element in place names, refers to the Native American population which once inhabited all of Colorado. **Indian Agency,** in La Plata County, is a postal station taking its name from the Southern Ute Indian Reservation. **Indian Creek,** in Teller County, takes its name from a nearby stream; there are twelve creeks so named in the state. **Indian Hills,** in Jefferson County (est. 1925), was founded by a realty firm as a summer resort; earlier, the area was known as Eaton Park. **Indian Meadows** is on Colorado 14 in Larimer County.

Indian Peaks is the name for a group of mountains on both sides of the Continental Divide in Grand and Boulder counties. Many peaks in this area are named after Indian tribes; from south to north, they are Arapaho, Arickaree, Kiowa, Navajo, Apache, Shoshone, Pawnee, and Paiute. The peak called Ute Mountain is not part of this group.

Iola [ī ō′ lə], in Gunnison County, was supposedly named by a rancher who thought the name had a pretty sound.

Ione [ī′ ōn], on U.S. 85 in Weld County. A story told of this name is that when W. A. Davis, owner of the townsite land, was asked by Union Pacific Railroad officials about the area, he said, "I own all the property around here"; so they thought "Ione" would be an appropriate name. However, Ione is also known as a woman's name, and as the name of an island off the coast of Scotland, famed as the residence of St. Columba.

Iris, in Saguache County, is supposedly named for the flower, *Iris missouriensis,* which is common in the area.

Irving Hale Creek and **Mount Irving Hale,** in Grand County (11,754 ft.). Named in 1915 for General Irving Hale (1862–1930), who led Colorado troops in the Spanish-American War, and who founded the Veterans of Foreign Wars.

Irwin, in Gunnison County, as well as **Irwin Lake,** were named for Dick Irwin, an early prospector in the area.

Ish Ranch, in Larimer County, was named for John and Mary Ish, who settled here in 1875.

Isolation Peak, on the Continental Divide between Grand and Boulder counties (13,118 ft.). Named in 1942 for its remote location.

Ivywild, in El Paso County (est. 1888). This Colorado Springs suburb was owned and platted by William B. Jenkins, and was named by his wife. The name was probably coined to suggest quiet surroundings.

Jack's Cabin, on Colorado 135 in Gunnison County, was named for John ("Jack") Howe, a local tavern keeper.

Jackson County (est. 1909, area 1,622 sq. mi., pop. 1,605). The county seat is Walden. The county was presumably named in honor of President Andrew Jackson (1767–1845); it was formed from a part of Larimer County. **Jackson Lake** is the name of bodies of water in Gunnison, Morgan, and Adams counties.

Jacque [zhäk] **Peak,** in Summit County (13,208 ft.). The name comes from John W. Jacque, a well-known mineowner in early Leadville and in the Ten Mile District (in which the mountain lies). He was sometimes called Captain Jacque, but it isn't known whether this was from Civil War service or from his profession as a "mining captain."

Jackstraw Mountain, in Rocky Mountain National Park, Grand County (11,704 ft.). Named in 1924 because dead trees on it, left jumbled after a fire in 1872, resembled the sticks in the children's game of jackstraws ("Pick Up Sticks").

James Peak, in Clear Creek County (13,294 ft.), was named around 1866 for Edwin James (1797–1861), who in 1820 was the first botanist to visit the Rocky Mountains. Separately named is **Jamestown,** a town in Boulder County (est. 1864, inc. 1883, pop. 251). While the post offfice, established in 1867, was called Jamestown, the camp seems to have originally been known as Jimtown—possibly for an early settler's nickname. Jimtown still is the name used in the locality. The mining camp was previously called Elysian Park, because of its beautiful mountain setting.

Jansen, on Colorado 12 in Las Animas County (est. 1900?). Probably named for Jansen's Quarry, which apparently became a settlement and station on the Santa Fe Railway and the Colorado and Southern Railroad. Previously known as Chimayoses.

Jaroso [hə rō′ sō], in Costilla County (est. 1914); also written "Jarosa," and pronounced [hə rō′ sə]. In the Spanish of New Mexico and Colorado, *jara* refers to the sandbar willow; thus *jaroso* means "covered with sandbar willows."

Jefferson, on U.S. 285 in Park County (est. 1861), was named for nearby **Jefferson Lake** and **Jefferson Creek,** which in turn honor President Thomas Jefferson (1743–1826). Originally two settlements, Palestine and Jefferson, they soon united under the latter name. Separately named is **Jefferson County** (est. 1861, area 783 sq. mi., pop. 438,430); the county seat is Golden. Named from "Jefferson Territory," the extralegal government which preceded Colorado Territory, and which also took its name from President Jefferson. It is one of the seventeen original territorial counties.

Joe Mills Mountain, in Rocky Mountain National Park, Larimer County (11,078 ft.). Named for Enoch Josiah ("Joe") Mills, brother of Enos Mills, and with him a creator of the National Park.

Joes, on U.S. 36 in Yuma County (est. 1912). Established by C. N. White and Joseph White. Among the settlers were three men named Joe; the place was first called Three Joes, and later shortened to its present form.

Johnson Village, on U.S. 24 and 285 in Chaffee County (est. 1947). Started as a cafe and service station by John Johnson at the U.S. 285 junction near Buena Vista.

Johnstown, town on Colorado 60 in Weld County (est. 1902, inc. 1907, pop. 1,579). Laid out by Harvey J. Parish, who named it for his son John.

Julesburg [jо̄о̄lz′ bûrg], town on U.S. 138 and 385 (est. 1884, inc. 1886, pop. 1,295); seat of Sedgwick County. Originally a stage station at the ranch and trading post of Jules Beni, from whom the town gets its name. The present town was located when the Union Pacific Railroad built a branch line to Denver. It was incorporated as Denver Junction in November, 1885, and as Julesburg the following year.

Julian, Mount, in Rocky Mountain National Park, Larimer County (12,928 ft.). Named for Julian Hayden, a civil engineer who settled in Estes Park in 1906.

Juniper Hot Springs, on the Yampa River in Moffat County. Named for the common juniper, *Juniperus communis,* a frequent plant in Colorado.

Jura [jōō´ rə] **Knob,** a mountain in San Juan County (12,614 ft.). Perhaps named for the Jura Mountains of France and Switzerland.

Kaibab [kī´ bab], in Eagle County (also pronounced [kī´ bäb]). From Ute *káava'avich* "mountain range," literally "mountain lying down," derived in turn from *kaav* "mountain." This is also the name of the Kaibab Plateau in Arizona and southern Utah.

Kannah [kan´ ə], on the Gunnison River in Mesa County; named after **Kannah Creek.** Perhaps from Ute *kanáv* "willow," or *kanáwiya* "a valley with willows."

Karval [kär´ vəl], in Lincoln County (est. 1910). Homesteaded in 1910 by Gulick K. Kravig, who became postmaster in 1911. The post office was first called Kravig, but this became confused with Craig. Kravig then suggested Karval—derived from Kars, the name of his home in Norway, plus "val," suggesting "valley."

Kassler, on Colorado 121 in Jefferson County (est. 1872?). The site of a Denver water-filter plant on the South Platte River, named for E. S. Kassler, president of the Denver Union Water Company from 1915 to 1918. Also known as Watertown after 1916.

Kawuneechee Valley [kä wōō nē´ chē], in Grand County. From an Arapaho word recorded in 1914 as Cawoonache, and said to mean "coyote." Evidently derived from *koo'óh* "wolf, coyote" plus *néechee* "chief."

Kebler [keb´ lər] **Pass,** in Gunnison County (9,980 ft.). Supposedly named for J. A. Kebler, an associate of the Redstone coal magnate, John C. Osgood.

Keenesburg, town in Weld County (est. 1907, inc. 1919, pop. 570). Originally a telegraph office and side track for the Chicago Burlington and Quincy Railroad, and named Keene after a rancher of the area. When a post office was established in 1907, the present name was suggested.

Kelim [kel′ əm], on U.S. 34 in Larimer County, was named for Lee J. Kelim, a pioneer in the Loveland area.

Kenosha [kə nō′ shə] **Pass,** in Park County (10,001 ft.), and nearby **Kenosha Peak** (12,429 ft.). Named for Kenosha, Wisconsin, by a stage coach driver who came from there. Supposedly the Chippewa (Algonkian) word for "pike" (the fish).

Keota [kē ō′ tə], town in Weld County (est. 1888, inc. 1919, pop. 5). Named for Keota, Iowa. The Iowa town was originally called Keoton, from being on the boundaries of Keokuk and Washington counties.

Keplinger Lake, in Boulder County. Named for L. W. Keplinger, the college student who accompanied Major John Wesley Powell on the first ascent of Longs Peak in 1868, and who was actually the person to reach the summit.

Kersey [kûr′ sē], town on Colorado 37 and U.S. 34 in Weld County (est. 1887, inc. 1908, pop. 980). With the building of the Union Pacific Railroad through here in 1882, a section house and station were erected and called Orr, in honor of James H. Orr, the first colonist to pay the $155 fee for Union Colony land. The name was often confused with Orr, California, and Carr, Colorado; so in 1896 it was renamed by Roadmaster John K. Painter, who gave it his mother's maiden name.

Keyser [kī′ zər] **Creek** is the name of streams in Garfield and Grand counties. Keyser is a common German and Dutch family name, originally meaning "emperor" and derived from Latin *Caesar.*

Kim, town on U.S. 160 in Las Animas County (est. 1918, inc. 1974, pop. 76). Named for the boy hero of Rudyard Kipling's novel *Kim.*

Kinikinik [kin′ i ki nik], on Colorado 14 in Larimer County. Named for an evergreen plant, usually spelled "kinnikinick," *Arctostaphylos uva-ursi.* The terms referred earlier to a combination of plant materials used for smoking, also called "killickinick," from a Delaware (Algonkian) word meaning "mixture."

Kiowa [kī′ ō wə], town on Colorado 86 (est. 1869, inc. 1912, pop. 275); seat of Elbert County. Named for the Kiowa Indian tribe of the southern Plains, who called themselves *kae-gua.* The tribal name is also applied to **Kiowa County** (est. 1889, area 1,767 sq. mi., pop. 1,688), of which the county seat is Eads. Formed from a portion of Bent County. **Kiowa Peak,** in Boulder County (13,276 ft.), is one of the Indian Peaks, named after tribes who formerly lived in and near Colorado.

Kirk, on Colorado 57 in Yuma County (est. 1883), was founded by A. Nekirk, and the town's name is an abbreviation of his.

Kit Carson [kit′ kär′ sən], town on U.S. 40 and 287 in Cheyenne County (est. 1869, inc. 1931, pop. 305). Named for the famous western scout and guide, Christopher ("Kit") Carson (1809–68). The original town was three miles west of its present site, on the banks of Sand Creek, and was the terminus of the Kansas Pacific Railroad. Carson's name was independently given to **Kit Carson County** (est. 1889, area 2,171 sq. mi., pop. 7,140), of which the county seat is Burlington. This unit was formed from a part of Elbert County. The same name is applied to **Kit Carson Peak,** in Saguache County (14,165 ft.), earlier called Haystack Baldy and Frustum Peak.

Kittredge, on Colorado 74 in Jefferson County (est. 1920). Originated when the Kittredge Town Company purchased the Luther Ranch of some three hundred acres. Charles M. Kittredge applied for a post office in 1921, suggesting it be called Bear Creek. There was already an office by that name, and postal officials decided to name the settlement for the Kittredge family, which had lived in the vicinity since 1860.

Kline, in La Plata County (est. 1904). The name was given by a Mormon colony that settled the town and established a post office; it may have been the name of a founder or a church leader. The community was eventually outgrown by the nearby settlement of Marvel. Mail for Marvel was received at Kline until 1953, when the post office was moved to Marvel.

Knobtop Mountain, in Rocky Mountain National Park, on the Continental Divide between Grand and Larimer counties (12,731 ft.). Named for its shape by Roger Toll in 1924, along with Flattop and Notchtop mountains.

Koen, in Prowers County, was named for Festus B. Koen and his brothers, who were early settlers.

Kokomo [kō kō′ mō], in Lake County, is named for a town in Indiana. The Indiana name is accented on the first syllable; it is said to have been the name of a local Indian.

Kornman, on U.S. 287 and 385 in Prowers County (est. 1908?). A station on the Atchison, Topeka and Santa Fe Railroad, named for Charles Kornman, a local landowner.

Kremmling [krem´ ling], town on U.S. 40 in Grand County (est. 1881, inc. 1904, pop. 1,166). The town's beginning was a general merchandise store run by Kare Kremmling, located on the Dr. Harris ranch on the north bank of the Muddy River. In 1888, John and Aaron Kinsey had part of their ranch platted, and called the site Kinsey City. Kremmling moved his store across the river to the new site, which soon became known as Kremmling.

KU [kā´ yoo´] **Gulch,** in Rio Blanco County, perhaps takes its name from a local ranch.

Kutch [kooch], in Elbert County (est. 1904). Named for Ira Kutch, a local cattleman. The first post office was established in 1878, under the name of Sanborn.

La Boca [lä bō´ kə], in La Plata County, is Spanish for "the mouth."

Lafayette [lä fä yet´], city on U.S. 287 in Boulder County (est. 1888, inc. 1890, pop. 14,548). Named for Lafayette Miller, husband of Mary E. Miller, owner of the townsite land.

La Fruto, on U.S. 285 in Alamosa County, stands for Spanish *la fruta* "the fruit."

La Garita [lä gə rē´ tə], in Saguache County (est. 1874?). Named for **La Garita Peak,** west of the town (13,710). Spanish for "the lookout." Reportedly Indians sent smoke signals from La Garita Peak to the Sangre de Cristo Range, across the San Luis Valley.

Laird, on U.S. 34 in Yuma County (est. 1887). Named for Congressman James Laird of Nebraska.

La Jara [lə hâr´ ə], town on U.S. 285 in Conejos County (est. 1880, inc. 1910, pop. 725). In the Spanish of New Mexico and Colorado, *jara* refers to the "sandbar willow," which grows along the banks of the **La Jara**

River. Before there were real settlements between the Conejos River and Rio Grande, a few Mexican families lived near this site, and the place was called *Llano Blanco* "white plain."

La Junta [lə hun′ tə], city on U.S. 50 and 350 (est. 1875, inc. 1881, pop. 7,637); seat of Otero County. Its name, Spanish for "the junction," refers to the joining of two railroad lines. The town was called Otero on Santa Fe Railway schedules during part of 1878.

Lake City, town on Colorado 149 (est. 1875, inc. 1884, pop. 223); seat of Hinsdale County. Name taken from nearby Lake San Cristobal (Spanish for "Saint Christopher"), one of the largest natural lakes in Colorado. It is the only community in the county, which is the state's least populous. Separately named is **Lake County** (est. 1861, area 379 sq. mi., pop. 6,007). The county seat is Leadville. Named for the Twin Lakes, outstanding features of the region. This is one of the original seventeen territorial counties, although its size has been diminished for creation of other counties. The community of Twin Lakes was once the county seat.

Lake Fork, a branch of the Conejos River, in Conejos County, is apparently named for Big Lake, through which it flows.

Lake George, on U.S. 24 in Park County (est. 1886). A pioneer rancher, George Frost, dammed the South Platte River as it came out of Eleven-Mile Canyon, to form a lake from which he cut ice for the Colorado Midland Railroad. First called Lidderdale Reservoir, it was commonly known as George's Lake. When a post office was established in 1891, it became Lake George. The ice business helped the community flourish, but died when the railroad was abandoned in 1918.

Lakeside, town in Jefferson County (est. 1907, inc. 1907, pop. 11). This tiny community, at West 46th Ave. and Sheridan Blvd., is the home of Lakeside Amusement Park. The site was named for its location around a small lake, now within the park.

Lakewood, city on Colorado 121 in Jefferson County (est. 1872, inc. 1969, pop. 126,481). Named for the many small lakes in the area. When the community was incorporated, it was already the third largest city in the state.

La Manga [lə mang′ gə] **Pass,** in Conejos County (10,230 ft.). Spanish for "the sleeve"; but in the Spanish of New Mexico and Colorado, the word can also refer to a narrow strip of land.

Lamar [lə mär´], city on U.S. 50, 287, and 385 (est. 1886, inc. 1886, pop. 8,343); seat of Prowers County. Named for Lucius Q. C. Lamar, the secretary of the interior at the time of its establishment.

La Plata [lə plat´ ə], in La Plata County (est. 1873). Named after the **La Plata Mountains,** between Montezuma and La Plata counties, and the **La Plata River;** the name contains the Spanish phrase meaning "the silver," because of silver discoveries by Spaniards in the eighteenth century. Also named after the mountain range and river is **La Plata County** (est. 1874, area 1,683 sq. mi., pop. 32,284); however, the county seat is not La Plata, but Durango. The unit was formed from portions of Conejos and Lake counties. The same name was given to **La Plata Peak,** in Chaffee County (14,336 ft.).

Laporte [lə pōrt´], on Colorado 14 in Larimer County (est. 1859). In 1858, John B. Provost and Antoine Janis, with a group of French trappers, came from the trading post at Fort Laramie to establish a new trading post, which they called Colona. The name was changed to its present form in 1862, when a post office was established. *La porte* is French for "the gate"; the name was given because the site is the natural gateway to the area lying to the northwest.

La Posta, in La Plata County, is Spanish for "stagecoach stop." It was a resting place for coaches between Durango and Farmington, New Mexico.

Laramie River, rising in Larimer County and running into Wyoming. Named for Jacques La Ramie, a French trapper who was killed by Indians near this stream around 1825.

Lariat [lâr´ ē et], in Rio Grande County. The English word for a noosed rope, used to catch livestock, was borrowed from Spanish *la reata.*

Larimer County (est. 1861, area 1,611 sq. mi., pop. 186,136). The county seat is Fort Collins. Named for General William Larimer, a founder of Denver. One of the original seventeen territorial counties. Most of the area of Rocky Mountain National Park is within the southwest part of the county.

Larkspur, town on Plum Creek and Colorado 18 in Douglas County (est. 1865, pop. 232). Named for the flower *Delphinium geyeri,* which is beautiful but poisonous to livestock.

La Salle [lə sal´], town on U.S. 85 in Weld County (est. 1910, inc. 1910, pop. 1,783). The existence of the town is supposed to be due to a quarrel between the Union Pacific Railroad and the city of Greeley. This led to La Salle's becoming the northern Colorado headquarters for the railroad in 1909 to 1910. The name may honor Robert Cavalier de La Salle (1643–87), the French explorer of the Mississippi River; or it may be transferred from La Salle, Illinois.

Las Animas [ləs an' i məs], city on U.S. 50 (est. 1869, inc. 1886, pop. 2,481); seat of Bent County. After the building of a new Fort Lyon, a flourishing settlement grew up on at the confluence of the Arkansas River and the stream which the Spanish called *Río de las Ánimas Perdidas en Purgatorio* "the river of lost souls in purgatory"—in English, the Purgatory River. When the Kansas Pacific Railroad built its branch from Kit Carson to the Arkansas River, the town of West Las Animas was settled six miles west of the first site. The name was changed to its present form in 1886. Farther upstream, the same name was given to **Las Animas County** (est. 1866, area 4,794 sq. mi., pop. 13, 765). The county seat is not Las Animas, but Trinidad. This is the largest of Colorado's sixty-three counties, but was originally a part of Huerfano County. The similarity to the name of the Animas River in southwestern Colorado is coincidental.

Lasauses [lə sô' səs], in Conejos County; also the name of a place in Costilla County. Also spelled Los Sauces; for Spanish *las sauces* "the willows."

Las Mesitas [läs mə sē' təs], on Colorado 17 in Conejos County. Spanish for "the little mesas."

Lascar [las' kər], in Huerfano County. The term means "an East Indian sailor," and was probably taken from a book; it has no local significance.

Last Chance, on U.S. 36 in Washington County (est. 1926). Established by Essa Harbert and Archie Chapman in the days of the Model T Ford. The name reflects the fact the site was the only place for many miles on U.S. 36 where one could obtain gas, oil, water, etc.

La Valley, in Costilla County, from Spanish *La* "the" plus English "valley."

La Veta [lə vē' tə], town on Colorado 12 in Huerfano County (est. 1876, inc. 1886, pop. 726). The Spanish name means "the vein," and probably refers here to the many dykes radiating in all directions from West Spanish Peak. It was formerly known as Francisco Plaza or Francisco Ranch, as Colonel John M. Francisco selected this site for his home while on a prospecting tour in 1834.

Lawson, on U.S. 6 and 40 in Clear Creek County (est. 1876). Once a solitary inn known as Six Mile House, owned by Alexander Lawson. When valuable ores were discovered here in 1876, many prospectors came and a town soon developed.

Lay, on U.S. 40 in Moffat County (est. 1880). After the Meeker Massacre (1879–80), soldiers were stationed at various points to protect supply trains on the road from Rawlins, Wyoming. A Lieutenant McCullough (or McCulloch) gave the name Camp Lay to one campsite, honoring his sweetheart in Chicago. The camp was abandoned; but the name was retained when a post office was later established.

Lazear [lə zēr´], in Delta County (est. 1910). Named for J. B. Lazear, a pioneer settler, after the town was founded by B. M. Stone as the supply point for the area's fruit and livestock districts.

Lead [led] **Mountain,** on the Continental Divide, between Jackson and Larimer counties (12,537 ft.). Named for the lead ore found here.

Leadville [led´ vil], city on U.S. 24 (est. 1878, inc. 1878, pop. 2,629); seat of Lake County. Silver strikes in this area were made in 1876 to 1877 and a rush began. The early camp was known by many names; Slabtown, Boughtown, Cloud City, Carbonate, Harrison, Agassiz. When the time came for legal adoption of a name, controversy raged. One faction favored Harrison, for the Harrison Reduction Works; but Horace Tabor, a storekeeper, favored Leadville, and prevailed. The name was chosen for the large amount of argentiferous lead ores in the vicinity.

Lebanon, in Montezuma County (est. 1908). Built in a dense setting of red cedars (*Juniperus scopulorum*), reminiscent of the biblical cedars of Lebanon.

Left Hand Creek, in Boulder County. Named for Andrew Sublette, a left-handed fur trader of the 1830s. It is coincidental that a nearby mountain and town bear the name of the Arapaho Chief Niwot, whose name means "left hand."

Lewis, in Montezuma County (est. 1909?). For W. R. Lewis, who purchased the townsite at the time the settlement was established.

Limon [lī´ mən], town on U.S. 24, 40, and 287 in Lincoln County (est. 1888, inc. 1909, pop. 1,831). The name resembles Spanish *limón* "lemon." One does not expect to find a subtropical fruit among Colorado place names;

however, *Limón* is also a Spanish surname. The town was established as a camp for the Rock Island Railroad; it was known as Limon's Camp, for the foreman, and later as Limon's Junction, for the meeting of the Rock Island and Union Pacific railroads. The spelling "Lyman Junction" is also recorded.

Lincoln County (est. 1889, area 2,593 sq. mi., pop. 4,529). The county seat is Hugo. Named in honor of President Abraham Lincoln (1809–65). The area was first traversed by goldseekers and later by stockmen, with homesteaders claiming acreage by the late 1890s. The county was formed from portions of Bent and Elbert counties. **Lincoln Park** is a community in Fremont County (pop. 3,728). **Mount Lincoln** is a peak in Park County (14,286 ft.). Wilbur F. Stone—then a placer miner, and later a noted jurist and Colorado historian—climbed the peak in 1861. When he asked fellow citizens to select a name appropriate for a magnificent mountain, the present name was the consensus. In 1864, miners of the area sent President Lincoln retorted gold valued at eight hundred dollars.

Lindon, on U.S. 36 in Washington County (est. 1888?). First known as Harrisburg. When the post office was moved three miles southeast, the name was changed to Linden, in honor of L. J. Lindbeck of Illinois, an early resident. The present spelling was adopted later.

Lindsey, Mount, in Costilla County (14,042 ft.). Named "Old Baldy" from the 1870s until 1954, when it was renamed after Malcolm Lindsey of Trinidad, a climber of the peak in his youth, and a prominent Denver attorney for much of his life.

Little Bear Creek, in Costilla County, gives its name to **Little Bear Peak,** in Costilla County (14,037 ft.), earlier called West Peak. It was first scaled in 1888.

Little Pisgah [piz′ gə] **Peak** is in Teller County (9,808 ft.). There are several Pisgah Peaks in Colorado; the name refers to the mountain from which Moses viewed the Promised Land.

Little Snake River is in Moffat County. There is no "Big Snake River," though a stream called Snake River exists in Summit County.

Little Thompson River, in Larimer County, like the neighboring Big Thompson River, may have been named for the English fur trapper, David Thompson (1770–1857), who explored the northern Rockies around 1810.

Littleton, city on U.S. 85 in Arapahoe and Douglas counties, and seat of Arapahoe County (est. 1872, inc. 1890, pop. 33,685). Founded by and named for Richard Sullivan Little, a civil engineer from New Hampshire, who came to Colorado in 1860 and started farming.

Livermore, on U.S. 287 in Larimer County (est. 1863). Named for two of the earliest permanent settlers, Adolphus Livernash and Stephen Moore, who built a cabin near the townsite and became prospectors.

Lizard Head Peak (13,113 ft.), between Dolores and San Miguel counties, takes its name from its peculiar shape. **Lizard Head Pass** (10,222 ft.) is nearby.

Lobatos [lə bä′ təs], in Conejos County, is perhaps the plural of the Spanish surname *Lobato*. The place was formerly called Cenicero "ash heap."

Lochbuie [lok bōō′ ē], town on U.S. 6 in Weld County (est. 1960, inc. 1974, pop. 1,168). Established first as Space City, then incorporated in 1974 as Lochbuie. The name Space City was derived from a house trailer court called Spacious Living. Lochbuie is the name of an area on the Isle of Mull in Scotland, where ancestors of one of the town's organizers lived.

Lodore [lə dōr′] **Canyon,** on the Green River in Moffat County. The name was suggested by Major John Wesley Powell, an early explorer of the Colorado River, who recalled the poem by Robert Southey, "The cataract of Lodore." The falls originally so named are in the Lake Country of England.

Logan is a locality in **Logan County** (est. 1887, area 1,822 sq. mi., pop. 17,567). The county seat is Sterling. The settlement and county were named for General John A. Logan (1826–86), who died shortly before the county was created from the eastern portion of Weld County.

Log Lane Village, town in Morgan County (est. 1955, inc. 1955, pop. 667). Earlier called Wahketa Village. First conceived as a site for a liquor store outside of "dry" Fort Morgan, and then expanded for a community. Originally every building, according to ordinance, was built from or sided with logs; but the ordinance was dropped in the mid-1960s.

Loma, on U.S. 6 in Mesa County (est. 1900?). Spanish for a "hill on a plain."

Lone Eagle Peak, in Grand County (11,920 ft.). Named in 1930 after the nickname of aviator Charles Lindbergh (1902–74).

Lonetree, in Archuleta County (est. 1895?). Probably named for a natural landmark. **Lone Tree Creek** is a name given to three streams in Colorado.

Longmont, city on U.S. 287 in Boulder County (est. 1871, inc. 1885, pop. 51,555) is named for its proximity to, and its splendid view of, **Longs Peak** (14,255 ft.). The mountain was named for Major Stephen H. Long, whose expedition of 1819 to 1820 explored the area which was to be Colorado. Longs Peak and Mount Meeker to the south were earlier known as the Two Ears (translating a French name) or the Two Guides (translated from the Arapaho).

Lorencito [lōr ən sē′ tō] **Canyon,** in Las Animas County, contains the Spanish nickname *Lorencito,* from *Lorenzo* "Lawrence."

Loretto [lōr et′ ō] **Heights,** an area in Denver, is named for a town in Italy, famous for its shrine to the Virgin Mary.

Los Cerritos [lôs sə rē′ təs], in Conejos County, is Spanish for "the little hills."

Los Fuertes [lôs fōō âr′ tās], in Costilla County, is Spanish for "the strong ones."

Los Mogotes [lôs mə gō′ tēs], a peak in Conejos County (9,818 ft.). In the Spanish of New Mexico and Colorado, *mogote* means a clump of trees standing isolated on a plain.

Los Pinos [lôs pē′ nəs], in Conejos County, is Spanish for "the pine trees"; a pronunciation closer to that of Spanish would be [lōs pē′ nōs]. **Los Pinos River,** also called Pine River, is in Hinsdale and La Plata counties. **Los Pinos Creek** and **Los Pinos Pass** (10,514 ft.) are in Saguache County.

Lottis Creek, in Gunnison County, was named in 1861 for Fred Lottis, a prospector.

Louisville [lōō′ is vil], city on Colorado 42 in Boulder County (est. 1878, inc. 1890, pop. 12,361); now sometimes pronounced [lōō′ ē vil], like the city in Kentucky. Coal was discovered here in 1877 by C. C. Welch of Golden. The boring was in charge of Louis Nowotny, who also owned the surface of the land on which the original settlement was located. Nowotny had the town platted, and his name was given to the settlement.

Louviers [loo′ vərz], in Douglas County (est. 1906). Founded as the site of an explosives factory of the Du Pont Company, and named for Louviers, Delaware, where the Du Ponts manufactured woolen cloth. The Delaware town, in turn, was named for a French city, the center of the woolen industry in France.

Loveland, city on U.S. 34 and 287 in Larimer County (est. 1877, inc. 1881, pop. 37,352). Named for William A. H. Loveland, president of the Colorado Central Railroad. The townsite was platted on the farm of David Barnes—later known as the "father of Loveland"—but he declined to have the town named for him. Also named for W. A. H. Loveland is **Loveland Pass,** on the Continental Divide between Clear Creek and Summit counties (11,990 ft.). The highway over this pass, U.S. 6, has been superseded by the Eisenhower Tunnel, on Interstate 70. **Loveland Heights** is on U.S. 34, near Estes Park, in Larimer County.

Lowry Field, an Air Force base in Denver, is named after Lieutenant Francis Brown Lowry, a native of Denver and aviator in World War I.

Lucerne [loo sûrn′], on U.S. 85 in Weld County (est. 1892?). When the Union Pacific Railroad built a side track and station, to load alfalfa and potatoes, the settlement was called Lucerne, the name by which alfalfa was formerly known.

Ludlow, in Las Animas County, was perhaps named for Ludlow, Massachusetts, which in turn was named after a town in England. The Colorado site is infamous for the "Ludlow Massacre" of 1914, when city and state militia were called to suppress a strike by coal miners.

Lulu City, in Rocky Mountain National Park, Grand County, is a former mining area. It was named for Lulu Burnett, daughter of Benjamin Franklin Burnett, a founder of the town. It is located on **Lulu Creek,** at the headwaters of the Colorado River. **Lulu Mountain** is on the Continental Divide, between Grand and Jackson counties (12,228 ft.).

Lycan [lī′ kən], on Colorado 89 and 116 in Baca County (est. 1910). Mabel Lycan and her Civil War veteran father, Morgan B. F. Tresner, homesteaded here in 1910. Their plan was to establish a community modeled after Tresner, Illinois, which had been settled by the Tresner family. The Colorado town was named by the settlers for Mrs. Lycan, who was the first school teacher, and was postmistress for twenty years.

Lyons, town on U.S. 36 in Boulder County (est. 1882, inc. 1891, pop. 1,227). Named for Mrs. Carrie Lyons, pioneer editor of the weekly *Lyons News,* published in 1890 to 1891.

Mack, on U.S. 6 in Mesa County (est. 1904). Founded by employees of the Uintah Railway, who named it for John M. Mack, builder of the railroad. The line was abandoned in 1939.

Madrid, on Colorado 12 in Las Animas County. Perhaps named for the city in Spain; but the word is also a Spanish family name.

Magnolia, in Boulder County, may have been named for a brand of whiskey. Beyond that the name refers to a flowering tree, native to the southeastern U.S., called after the French botanist Pierre Magnol (1638–1715).

Mahana [mə hä′ nə] **Peak,** in Rocky Mountain National Park, Boulder County (12,632 ft.). Ellsworth Bethel wanted to name this Comanche Peak, as part of the Indian Peaks group. But the U.S. Board on Geographic Names, doubtless noting that a peak thirty-five miles to the north had borne the name Comanche since the 1876 King Survey, rejected his suggestion. Bethel then substituted Mahana, supposedly the name by which the Comanche were called by the Taos Indians of New Mexico.

Maher [mā′ hər], on Colorado 92 in Montrose County (est. 1882); also pronounced [mā′ ər]. For Caleb Maher, who was the first stage driver in the vicinity, and in 1884 became the first postmaster.

Malta, in Lake County (est. 1876). Named for the Malta Smelting Works, established to extract lead from ore which was brought from the Leadville area. The smelter may have taken its name from the island of Malta in the Mediterranean Sea.

Manassa [mə nas′ ə], town on Colorado 142 in Conejos County (est. 1879, inc. 1899, pop. 988). When settled by Mormon colonists, Elder Lawrence M. Peterson suggested the biblical name Manassa (also spelled Manasseh), in honor of the eldest son of Joseph. The town is noted as the home town of William Harrison ("Jack") Dempsey, the "Manassa Mauler," world heavyweight boxing champion, 1919 to 1926.

Mancos [mang´ kəs], town on U.S. 160 in Montezuma County (est. 1881, inc. 1894, pop. 842). Named for the **Mancos River** (also in Montezuma County). The plural of Spanish *manco* "one-handed, faulty, crippled."

Manhattan, in Larimer County. Perhaps after the island in New York City, named for the Indian tribe which inhabited it.

Manitou [man´ i to͞o] **Park,** in Teller County. The name is an Algonkian word for "spirit." The word also occurs in the name of **Manitou Springs,** a city on U.S. 24 in El Paso County (est. 1871, inc. 1888, pop. 4,535). First called Villa La Font (Fountain Village), the town was soon renamed Manitou. In 1885 it became Manitou Springs, but reverted to Manitou again in 1892, and in 1935 took its present name, Manitou Springs.

Manti-La Sal [man´ tē lə sal´] **National Forest,** in Mesa and Montrose counties, has its headquarters in Manti, Utah; this town is named after a city in the Book of Mormon. The La Sal Mountains, also in Utah, are named with Spanish *la sal* "the salt," because of salt deposits in the area.

Manzanares [man zə när´ əs] **Creek,** in Huerfano County. Plural of Spanish *manzanar* "apple orchard."

Manzanola [man zə nō´ lə], town on U.S. 50 in Otero County (est. 1900, inc. 1900, pop. 437). First settled in 1869, and called Catlin. It was incorporated under that name in 1891, but reincorporated as Manzanola in 1900. The name is evidently coined after Spanish *manzana* "apple," because of the local orchards.

Marble, town in Gunnison County (est. 1880?, inc. 1889, pop. 64). Named for the large marble deposits along Yule Creek, south of the town. The Yule marble was used for the Lincoln Memorial and the Tomb of the Unknown Soldier in Washington, D.C.

Marmot Point, a peak in Rocky Mountain National Park, Larimer County (12,041 ft.). The name refers to the yellow-bellied marmot, *Marmoth flaviventris,* the animal called "groundhog" or "woodchuck" in other parts of the U.S.

Maroon Bells, in Pitkin County, refers to two peaks, formerly collectively named Maroon Mountain. They are now called **South Maroon Peak**

(14,156 ft.) and **North Maroon Peak** (14,014 ft.). Named for their coloration by the Hayden Survey, these are said to be the most photographed peaks in Colorado, and are often used as calendar art. **Maroon Creek** and **Lake** are in Pitkin County. **East Maroon Pass,** at 11,800 feet, and **West Maroon Pass,** at 12,400 feet, are between Pitkin and Gunnison counties.

Marshall, on Colorado 93 in Boulder County (est. 1878). A one-time business center for a rich coal mining territory, the settlement was founded by Joseph M. Marshall, who discovered coal here. The post office name was changed in 1882 to Langford—probably for N. P. Langford, president of the Marshall Coal Company—the settlement continued to be known as Marshall. **Marshall Creek,** in Saguache County, as well as **Marshall Pass** (on the Continental Divide), were named after Lieutenant William L. Marshall, who discovered the pass in 1873.

Marten Peak, in Grand County (12,041 ft.). Named for the pine marten, *Martes americana,* related to the weasel.

Marvel, on the Southern Ute Reservation in La Plata County (est. 1915). Established on the homestead of John H. Miller, who ran a grocery and general store. The name was taken from a cooperative flour mill named the Marvel Midget.

Masonville, in Larimer County (est. 1875). Once an important trading post, it was settled by Benjamin, James, and Joseph Miller, and named for James R. Mason, a rancher who laid out the site when gold was discovered nearby. When a post office was established in 1880, postal authorities changed the name to Masonville to avoid confusion with another place called Mason.

Massive, Mount, in Lake County (14,421 ft.). Just twelve feet shorter than its neighbor and number one peak, Mount Elbert, this mountain was named for its size in 1873 by Henry Gannett, a member of the Hayden exploring party. Around 1965 there was an unsuccessful move to rename the peak Mount Churchill, after the British prime minister of the World War II period.

Masters, in Weld County (post office est. 1900). Named by John Barton, owner of the 4-Bar Cattle Ranch, for his foreman, John Masters.

Matheson, on U.S. 24 in Elbert County (est. 1886). Named for Duncan Matheson, an early day sheepman upon whose land the town was built.

Maybell, on U.S. 40 in Moffat County (post office est. 1884). The first post office in this vicinity was at the Bell & Banks ranch, and was named for Bell's wife, May.

Mayday, in La Plata County (est. 1890?). Named for the Mayday Mine, established near Mayday Junction on the Rio Grande Southern Railroad.

McClave, on Colorado 196 in Bent County (est. 1906?). Named for B. T. McClave, owner of the townsite land. The settlement grew up around a beet dump of the American Beet Sugar Company.

McClure Pass, between Gunnison and Pitkin counties (8,755 ft.). For Thomas McClure, noted as the developer of the Red McClure potato.

McCoy, on Colorado 131 in Eagle County (est. 1890). Settled and named by Charles H. McCoy, a rancher who became the first postmaster in 1891.

McGregor, on U.S. 40 in Routt County. Independently named is **McGregor Mountain,** in Rocky Mountain National Park, Larimer County (10,486 ft.), which honors Alexander Q. MacGregor, a lawyer from Milwaukee who settled in Estes Park in 1876.

McPhee Park, in Montezuma County, a virgin stand of yellow ponderosa pine set aside in 1925. Suppposedly named for C. D. McPhee, of the McPhee Lumber Company in Denver, who once operated a lumber mill there.

Mead, town in Weld County (est. 1905, inc. 1908, pop. 456). Dr. Martin S. Mead homesteaded here about 1886. When the Great Western Sugar Company built a spur and beet dump here, Louis Roman and Paul Mead (a son of the doctor) founded the town and named it in Dr. Mead's honor.

Medano [mad′ ə nō] **Creek,** in Saguache County; also pronounced [med′ ə nō]. From Spanish *médano* "sand dune."

Medicine Bow Mountains, between Jackson and Larimer counties, extending north into Wyoming. In English as used by American Indians, "medicine" frequently means "supernatural power," and a medicine bow is used to invoke such power. The mountains were named after the Medicine Bow River in Wyoming, but it is not clear why the river received such a name.

Meeker, town on Colorado 13 (est. 1882, inc. 1885, pop. 2,098), seat of Rio Blanco County. Named for Nathan C. Meeker, a founder of the city of

Greeley. While he was U.S. Indian agent at White River in November, 1879, he and his employees were murdered by Indians; Meeker's wife and daughter and another woman were carried away as captives. After this massacre, a military post called "Camp on White River" was established four miles above the ruined agency. When this was abandoned in 1883, all the buildings were sold to the residents of the valley, who thus acquired a ready-made town. **Meeker Park,** on Colorado 7 in Boulder County (est. 1900?) is probably for nearby **Mount Meeker** (13,911 ft.), also named for Nathan Meeker.

Mendicant Ridge, in Gunnison County (11,425 ft.). Said to be named for an old prospector who frequented this region, begging flour and tobacco from Indians and whites.

Mendota Peak, in Ouray County (13,275 ft.). A Spanish family name.

Meredith, on the Fryingpan River in Pitkin County (est. 1900). Named by A. E. Beard, apparently a town founder, after a personal friend.

Merino [mə rē′ nō], town on U.S. 6 in Logan County (est. 1874, inc. 1917, pop. 238). Originally known as Buffalo. In 1882 the Union Pacific Railroad cut-off was built, and railroaders renamed the town for the huge flocks of Merino sheep raised there.

Mesa [mā′ sə], on Colorado 65 (est. 1887?). Located in **Mesa County** (est. 1883, area 3,301 sq. mi., pop. 93,145), formed out of Gunnison County; the county seat is not Mesa, but Grand Junction. Both the town and the county are named with the Spanish word meaning "table," and by extension "table land" or "plateau." The term is also used in the **Mesa,** a locality in El Paso County. It also forms part of the name of many geographical features in Colorado, but frequently in combinations that would be ungrammatical in Spanish. That is, Anglo usage combines *mesa,* a feminine noun, with following masculine adjectives; thus **Mesa Cortado** [kōr tä′ də], a prominence in Archuleta County (8,556 ft.), stands for *mesa cortada* "chopped-off mesa." **Mesa Inclinado** [in kli nä′ də], a prominence in Montrose County (7,740 ft.), means "sloping mesa." **Mesa Lato** [lä′ tə], a prominence in Hinsdale County (12,675 ft.), means "broad mesa." **Mesa Pedregona,** a prominence in Archuleta County (8,172 ft.), is "rocky mesa." **Mesa Seco,** a prominence in Hinsdale County (12,800 ft.), means "dry mesa." **Mesa Verde** [vâr′ dā] **National Park,** in Montezuma County, refers to a "green mesa"; more old-fashioned pronunciations are [vûr′ dē] or [vûrd].

Mesita [mə sē′ tə], in Costilla County (est. 1909?), is Spanish for "small mesa," referring to a nearby hill. The settlement was first called Hamburg, but was changed to avoid confusion with a similarly named town.

Messex, on U.S. 6 in Washington County. Said to be named for Joe Messex, an early day railroader, who was killed while at work in the vicinity.

Mestas, Mount, in Huerfano County (11,569 ft.). Spanish *mesta* refers to an association of livestock owners.

Michigan River, in Jackson County, a tributary of the North Platte River. Named after the state; the term means "great lake" in an Algonkian language.

Middle Park, the valley of Muddy Creek in Grand County, one of the large inter-mountain valleys of Colorado named by early fur trappers. So called for its position between North Park (drained by the North Platte River) and South Park (in the South Platte drainage).

Midway, in Gunnison County, so called because it is half way between the settlements of Vulcan and Spencer. There is also a Midway in Teller County, and another on U.S. 34 in Larimer County.

Milliken, town on Colorado 60 in Weld County (est. 1909, inc. 1910, pop. 1,605). In honor of John D. Milliken, president of the Southwestern Land & Iron Company.

Mills Lake, in Rocky Mountain National Park, Larimer County. Named after Enos Mills, an early settler who worked for the establishment of the national park.

Milner, on U.S. 40 in Routt County (est. 1917). Named for a pioneer banker and merchant of the area. **Milner Pass,** on the Continental Divide between Grand and Larimer counties (10,758 ft.), is probably named for T. J. Milner, an early day civil engineer for railroads and streetcar lines.

Mineral County (est. 1893, area 921 sq. mi., pop. 558). The county seat is Creede. Its name, and existence, reflect to the many mineral resources of the region. Rich silver ores were discovered in 1890 by Nicholas Creede, for whom the county seat is named. Portions of Saguache and Rio Grande counties made up the new county.

Mineral Hot Springs, on Colorado 17 in Saguache County (est. 1880), homesteaded in 1880 by Sylvester A. Jenks. The thirty-seven medicinal springs were named in 1912 by Everett Dunshee, whose father owned the site at that time.

Minnehaha, on Ruxton Creek in El Paso County. Named for the heroine of Longfellow's *Hiawatha*. Originally a combination of Siouan words meaning "water" and "falls," but misinterpreted to mean "laughing waters."

Minnequa [min´ i kwä], in Pueblo County. May contain the Siouan word for "water."

Minnesota Creek, in Gunnison County; also **Minnesota Pass** (9,992 ft.). Named for the state, which was in turn called after the Minnesota River, from Dakota (Siouan) *mní^n sóta* "cloudy water."

Minturn, town on U.S. 24 in Eagle County (est. 1885, inc. 1904, pop. 1,066). For Thomas Minturn, a Denver and Rio Grande Western Railroad roadmaster.

Miramonte, in Boulder County. Modeled on Spanish *mirar* "to look at" plus *monte* "mountain," in the sense of "mountain view."

Mishawaka [mish ə wä´ kə], on Colorado 14 in Larimer County. Probably named after Mishiwaka, Indiana, a Potawatomi (Algonkian) name meaning "dead trees place."

Missouri Mountain, in Chaffee County (14,067 ft.). Because it was connected by ridges to neighbors Mount Oxford and Mount Belford, Missouri was not known as a separate mountain until 1956, when the U.S. Geological Survey gave it a separate identity and elevation. The name stems from the state of Missouri, which is called after the river, which was named in turn after the Algonkian name for a tribe living at its mouth.

Model, on U.S. 350 in Las Animas County (est. 1900?). First called Poso, from Spanish *pozo* "well," then changed to Roby. The name was changed again in 1920, when plans were made to develop the community as a "model town," with its own irrigation district and platted townsite.

Moffat, town on Colorado 17 in Saguache County (est. 1890, inc. 1911, pop. 99). Laid out by the San Luis Town & Improvement Association when the narrow-gauge Denver and Rio Grande Railroad was built into the region. The town was named for David H. Moffat, president of the railroad. Independently named for David Moffat was **Moffat County** (est. 1911, area 4,743 sq. mi., pop. 11,357); the county seat is Craig. The county was created from part of Routt County. **Moffat Tunnel,** a railway tunnel completed under the Continental Divide in 1927, between Gilpin County and Grand County, was also named after the rail executive; it shortened the run from Denver to Salt Lake City by 175 miles.

Mogote [mə gō´ tē], on Colorado 17 in Conejos County. Named for the nearby mountain peaks called Los Mogotes. In the Spanish of New Mexico and Colorado, *mogote* refers to a clump of trees standing isolated in a plain.

Molas [mō´ ləs] **Pass,** in San Juan County (10,910 ft.), is named for nearby **Molas Lake.** The lake in turn is supposedly named for so-called "moles," groundhog-like animals of the vicinity, presumably through a Spanish form *molas*. The trouble is that "mole," the animal, is called *topo* in Spanish, not *mola*. There is a Spanish word *mola* which corresponds to a different English word "mole," meaning "a fleshy mass in the uterus." It's possible that the lake was named by an Anglo who looked up the word "mole" in a Spanish-English dictionary, and came up with the wrong Spanish term. Or the name may be a corruption of Spanish *mulas* "mules."

Molina [mō lē´ nə], on Colorado 330 in Mesa County (est. 1883?). First known as Orson, after the postmaster; but when he, because of some difficulty, was asked to leave town, the office was renamed Snipes in honor of his successor. The present name, Spanish for "mill," was given after a water-powered flour mill was built nearby on Cottonwood Creek.

Monarch, a ski resort on U.S. 50 in Chaffee County, takes its name from **Monarch Pass,** on the Continental Divide, between Chaffee and Gunnison counties (11,312 ft.). The name was previously given to a mining camp of the 1880s, located near the present limestone quarry operations on the east side of the pass. **Monarch Lake,** in Grand County, is named for the Monarch Gold & Copper Mining & Smelting Company, founded in 1903.

Montana Mountain, in Gilpin County (10,948 ft.), probably reflects Spanish *montaña* "mountain," and hence means literally "Mountain Mountain."

Montbello, a section of northeast Denver, is from Italian *monte bello* "beautiful mountain."

Montclair, a postal station and neighborhood in Denver, is French for "clear mountain." It was originally designed as a spa by Baron Walter von Richthofen.

Monte Vista [mon´ tə vis´ tə], city on U.S. 160 and 285 in Rio Grande County (est. 1886, inc. 1886, pop. 4,324). Mock-Spanish for "mountain view"; more correct would be *vista del monte.* Sometimes called "Monte" for short. Prior to 1886, when it was formally platted and incorporated, the town was called Lariat, and later Henry.

Montezuma, town on the Snake River in Summit County (est. 1865, pop. 60). An early silver camp, named for the Aztec emperor of Mexico who ruled from 1503 to 1520. Separately named is **Montezuma County** (est. 1889, area 2,094 sq. mi., pop. 18,672), formed from a section of La Plata County; the county seat is Cortez. The prehistoric dwellings in Montezuma County were once thought, erroneously, to have been built by the Aztecs. **Montezuma Peak** is in Archuleta County (13,150 ft.).

Montrose, city on U.S. 50 and 550 (est. 1882, inc. 1882, pop. 8,854); seat of **Montrose County** (est. 1883, area 2,238 sq. mi., pop. 24,423), which was formed from a portion of Gunnison County. The county is named for the town, which in turn was named by its founder, Joe Selig, for the Dutchess of Montrose in Scott's *Legend of Montrose* (1819).

Monument, town in El Paso County (est. 1874, inc. 1881, pop. 1,020). Named for a rock formation west of the town. At the time of its founding, there were two post offices in the county with similar names. To untangle the mix-up, Monument Station, named because of its proximity to **Monument Park,** was renamed Edgerton. The other post office named Monument (called Henry Station by the Denver and Rio Grande Railroad) then kept Monument as its official name. **Monument Lake,** a reservoir in Las Animas County, was named for a natural stone obelisk left standing in the water after a dam was constructed. From this was named the settlement of **Monument Lake Park** (est. 1927?).

Moqui [mō´ kē] **Canyon,** in Montezuma County, uses a name applied to the Hopi Indian tribe of Arizona.

Morapos [mōr ap´ əs] **Creek,** in Moffat County. Locally said to have been named "Moor Rapids" by T. H. Iles, because the landscape reminded him of Scottish moors. However, the word may also be from Ute *murápuch* "something big."

Morgan, in Conejos County, is named separately from **Morgan County** (est. 1889, area 1,278 sq. mi., pop. 21,939), formed out of Weld County. The county was named for its seat, Fort Morgan, orginally established in 1865 to 1868 as protection against the Indians.

Morley, on U.S. 85 and 87 in Las Animas County. Perhaps named for Tom Morley, a local coal mine owner; or for William R. Morley, a construction engineer for the Santa Fe Railroad, who laid out the rail line here in 1879.

Morrison, town on Colorado 8 in Jefferson County (est. 1872, inc. 1906, pop. 465). Named for George Morrison, an 1859 pioneer, who home-steaded the townsite land.

Mosca [mos′ kə, mōs′ kə], in Alamosa County (est. 1890?). Named after **Mosca Pass,** which lies to the east, between Alamosa and Huerfano counties. For a few years the town was known as Orean, but the name reverted to Mosca. Spanish *mosca* means "fly"; however, the place name supposedly honors Luis Moscoso de Alvarado, successor in command of De Soto's exploration party after De Soto's death in 1542.

Mosquito Creek is the name of six streams in the state. In addition, **Mosquito Peak** lies between Lake and Park counties (13,782 ft.). Also nearby is **Mosquito Pass** (13,186 ft.).

Mountain View, town in Jefferson County (est. 1904, inc. 1904, pop. 550), was named for the prospect of the Rockies to the west. There are places with the same name in Larimer and Montrose counties.

Mount Crested Butte, town in Gunnison County (est. 1974, inc. 1974, pop. 274). Named for the nearby mountain, resembling a cock's comb.

Mount of the Holy Cross, in Eagle County (14,005 ft.). Named for the huge cross of snow—1,400-foot tall, about 450-foot wide—in crevices on its east face. First photographed by William H. Jackson in 1873, and painted by artist Thomas Moran later, it became almost as famous as Pikes Peak. Crumbling rocks have caused the cross to lose some of its outline. President Hoover proclaimed the area around the peak a national monument in 1929.

Mount Princeton Hot Springs, a locale in Chaffee County (est. 1875?), lies in the shadow of **Mount Princeton** (14,197 ft.). The peak, in turn, as one of the "Collegiate" group, is named for the university in Princeton, New Jersey.

Muckawanago [muk ə wä′ nə gō] **Creek,** in Pitkin County. Probably from a Wisconsin place name "Mukwanago," said to be an Algonkian word for "bear-lair."

Muddy Pass, on the Continental Divide, between Grand and Jackson counties (8,772 ft.). Named for **Muddy Creek,** a tributary of the Colorado River, which probably got its name when its waters were roiled by a storm. Twelve other streams in the state are called Muddy Creek.

Mummy Mountain, in Rocky Mountain National Park, Larimer County (13,425); also the **Mummy Range** and **Mummy Pass.** Supposedly the range resembles an Egyptian mummy lying on its back. "Its name was derived from an alleged resemblance requiring an active imagination to perceive," wrote historian Jerome Smiley in 1901.

Mustang Creek is a name given to four streams in Colorado. The English word for a wild horse is borrowed from Spanish *mesteño*.

Mystic, in Routt County. Supposedly named after Mystic, Iowa, by Fred May, an early settler who came from there. The name came earlier from Mystic, Connecticut. The name is orginally Algonkian, said to mean "big (tidal) river."

Nakai [nā′ kī] **Peak,** in Grand County (12,216 ft.), seems to reflect the fashion for giving Indian names to mountains in this area; it is probably the Navajo word *naakaii* "Mexican."

Nanita [nə nē′ tə] **Lake,** in Rocky Mountain National Park, Grand County. Perhaps from a Navajo word referring to the Plains Indians, or it may be a name used for the Comanches by a tribe of Texas Indians.

Narraguinnep [når ə gwin′ əp] **Canyon,** in Dolores County. Probably from Ute *náragwinap* "battleground."

Nathrop [nā′ thrəp], on the Arkansas River in Chaffee County (est. 1880). The original town, about a mile and a half above the present site, was known as Chalk Creek. It moved south in 1880 when the Denver and Rio Grande Railroad reached here. The site of the new settlement was owned in part by Charles Nachtrieb, a pioneer merchant and freighter;

and the town was named for him—Nathrop being a corruption of his name. He was murdered in Nathrop in 1881.

Naturita [nat yōō rē′ tə], town on Colorado 141 in Montrose County (est. 1882, inc. 1951, pop. 820). Named after nearby **Naturita Creek,** apparently a diminutive of Spanish *natura* "nature."

Navajo [nav′ ə hō] **Peak,** on the Continental Divide, between Grand and Boulder counties (13,409 ft.). Named in accord with Ellsworth Bethel's suggestions for naming a group of mountains, the so-called Indian Peaks, after Native American tribes. The tribal name is from Spanish *Navajó,* orginally a place name, borrowed from Tewa *nava-huu* "field-valley." There is a **Navajo River** in Archuleta County.

Nebo [nē′ bō], **Mount,** in San Juan County (13,205 ft.), is named for the biblical mountain from which Moses viewed the Promised Land (also known as Mount Pisgah).

Nederland [ned′ ər lənd], town on Colorado 119 in Boulder County (est. 1877, inc. 1885, pop. 1,099). Known as Brownsville in 1870, later as Middle Border or Tungsten Town. It was closely associated with the Caribou silver mines, which were purchased by Dutch investors; *Nederland* is Dutch for the "Netherlands."

Neegronda [nē gron′ də] **Reservoir,** in Kiowa County. The name is from a Siouan language, probably Osage *ni^{n} kdha^{n}dhe* "broad water." It is not clear why this and other lakes in Kiowa County were given Osage names, since the Osage tribe lived farther to the east.

Neenoshe [nē nō′ shə] **Reservoir,** in Kiowa County. Apparently from Osage *ni^{n} ozho* "principal water"; perhaps from the same source as the town of Neosho in Missouri.

Neeskah [nē′ skə] **Reservoir,** in Kiowa County. From Osage *ni^{n} ska* "white water."

Neesopah [nē sō′ pä] **Reservoir,** in Kiowa County. Perhaps from Osage *ni^{n} shüpe* "entrails water."

Neoga [nē ō′ gə] **Mountain,** in Hinsdale County (10,902 ft.). Perhaps named for Neoga, Illinois—a name of obscure origin.

Neota [nē ō´ tə], **Mount,** on the Continental Divide between Larimer and Grand counties (11,734 ft.); said to be an abbreviation of Arapaho *hóho'éniinóte' hítee* "mountain sheep's heart."

Nepesta [nə pes´ tə], on U.S. 50 in Pueblo County. From the Spanish name for the Arkansas River, *Río Nepesta,* derived in turn from an unknown Indian source.

Neva, Mount, on the Continental Divide between Grand and Boulder counties (12,814 ft.). Also written as Nevo. Said to have been named by Ellsworth Bethel for an Arapaho chief, an associate of Chief Niwot.

Never Summer Mountains, in Jackson and Grand counties. A translation of the Arapaho name for the range, referring to the permanent snows.

New Castle, town on U.S. 6 in Garfield County (est. 1884, inc. 1890, pop. 679). Known as Grand Butte in 1866, and as Chapman in 1867. In 1888, after the discovery of large bituminous coal fields, it was renamed by the Colorado Fuel & Iron Company for Newcastle, a famous mining center in England.

New Raymer, name of the post office at Raymer, in Weld County; given to avoid confusion with Ramah, in El Paso County.

Nimbus, Mount, on the Continental Divide between Jackson and Grand counties (12,706 ft.). This is one of several peaks in this area named after cloud formations; a nimbus is a gray rain cloud covering the sky.

Ninaview [nī´ nə vyōō], in Bent County (est. 1915). Named for Nina, the wife of T. R. Jones, on whose ranch the post office stood. Postal authorities added the word "view," forming the present name.

Nisa [nē´ sə], **Mount,** in Grand County (10,788 ft.). Named by Ellsworth Bethel from Arapaho *nîissóo* "twin," because of the double peak.

Niwot [nī´ wot], on Colorado 119 in Boulder County (est. 1872, pop. 2,666). Founded by W. T. Wilson, and first called Modoc. It was changed to Ni-Wot in 1879, honoring the Indian chief Niwot or Nawat; his name is probably from Arapaho *noowôothinoo* "I am left-handed." This Indian leader was esteemed by early settlers for his honesty and friendliness. **Niwot Mountain,** in the Indian Peaks area, Boulder County (11,471 ft.), was named in later years for the same chief. But Lefthand Creek, in the same area, was named years earlier for Andrew Sublette, a left-handed fur trader of the 1830s.

Nokhu [nō´ ko͞o] **Crags,** in Jackson County (12,485 ft.). Dramatic rock projections, the northernmost peaks of the Never Summer Range. Probably an abbreviation of Arapaho *hoh'onóókee* "eagle rock."

Nokoni [nō kō´ nē], **Lake,** in Rocky Mountain National Park, Grand County. Said to be the name of a Comanche band; the literal meaning is "traveling in a circle."

No Name Creek is the name of seven streams in Colorado. The same appelation is given to a draw, three gulches, a lake, and a ridge.

Northglenn, city on U.S. 87 in Adams County (est. 1959, inc. 1969, pop. 27,195). The name refers to the fact that the site is north of Denver. The developers later opened a shopping center south of Denver, labeled Southglenn.

North Park, valley of the North Platte River in Jackson County. The northernmost of the large inter-mountain valleys of Colorado named by early fur traders and trappers.

North Pass, on the Continental Divide, in Saguache County (10,149 ft.). Also called North Cochetopa Pass. The original Cochetopa pass, to the south, was once an Indian and buffalo trail between the San Luis Valley and the Gunnison area.

North Platte River, rising in Jackson County and flowing northward into Wyoming. It eventually turns eastward into Nebraska, where it joins the South Platte River. From French *Rivière Platte,* earlier Spanish *Río Chato* "flat river," because of its shallowness: "a mile wide and an inch deep."

North Pole, in El Paso County (est. 1956). Founded as a commercial tourist attraction, the site of "Santa's Workshop."

Norwood, town on Colorado 145 in San Miguel County (est. 1885, inc. 1903, pop. 429). Named for a community in Missouri by its founder, I. M. Copp.

Notchtop Mountain, in Rocky Mountain National Park, Larimer County (12,129 ft.). The name, reflecting the shape of the peak, was suggested by Dr. William J. Workman; cf. Knobtop, Gabletop, and Flattop Mountains in the same area.

Nucla [nōō´ klə], town in Montrose County (est. 1904, inc. 1915, pop. 656). Established by the Colorado Cooperative Company as a socialistic colony. The name, suggested by C. E. Williams, is based on "nucleus," meaning a center. It was chosen because the colonists believed their socialistic form of government would spread over the nation, and that their town would be the center of the movement.

Numa, in Crowley County. Numa Pompilius was the second king of Rome, the successor of the founder Romulus.

Nunn, town on U.S. 85 in Weld County (est. 1904, inc. 1908, pop. 324). Named for Tom Nunn, homesteader, who prevented a serious train wreck by flagging a train after he discovered a burning bridge near Pierce. As a token of its appreciation, the Union Pacific Railroad built a house for Nunn. About 1904, when a switch was built by the railroad, John Peterson, section foreman, suggested it be named for Nunn. The town previously had been known as Maynard.

Nutria, on U.S. 160 in Archuleta County. From the New Mexican Spanish word for "beaver"; in standard Spanish, it means "otter."

Nymph Lake, in Rocky Mountain National Park, Larimer County. Named in the 1920s for the yellow pond lily, discovered in Boulder County in 1864 and then called *Nymphae polysepala*. The genus name was later changed to *Nuphar.*

Oak Creek, town on Colorado 131 in Routt County (est. 1907, inc. 1907, pop. 673). Named for the creek upon which it lies; but there are six other streams named **Oak Creek** in Colorado. Only one species of oak is native to Colorado: the scrub oak, *Quercus gambelii.*

Ogalalla [ō gə lä′ lə] **Peak,** on the Continental Divide between Grand and Boulder counties (13,138 ft.). Named for a division of the Teton Sioux Indian tribe; the native name is *oglála,* said to mean literally "they scatter their own."

Oh-Be-Joyful Creek, Pass, and **Peak,** in Gunnison County. Perhaps from a once popular song, "Oh, won't it be joyful."

Ohio, on Quartz Creek in Gunnison County (est. 1880). Named for the state, and in turn for the river. Ohio is an Iroquois word meaning "beautiful river." The community experienced two booms—when minerals were first discovered in Colorado, and again in 1899, as the center of a gold producing district. Nearby are an **Ohio Pass** (10,033 ft.) and **Ohio Peak** (12,271 ft.). There is another **Ohio Peak** in San Juan County (12,673 ft.).

Ojito [ō hē′ tō], the Spanish diminutive of *ojo* "eye; spring (of water)," refers to a small spring. The term occurs in a number of place names in southern Colorado; thus **Ojito Banadero** [bän yə dâr′ ō], a spring in Las Animas County, is for *ojito bañadero* "spring for bathing." **Ojito Creek** is the name of two streams in Conejos and Costilla counties, and **Ojito Peak** is in Costilla County (10,458 ft.).

Ojo [ō′ hō], the Spanish word for "eye," also means "a spring of water," and is found in many place names. **Ojo de Alamo** [dā al′ ə mō], in Huerfano County, is from Spanish *ojo de álamo* "cottonwood spring." **Ojo Negro** [nā′ grō], a spring in Las Animas County, means "black spring." **Ojo Verde** [vâr′ dā], in Las Animas County, refers to a "green spring."

Oklahoma, Mount, on the Continental Divide between Pitkin and Lake counties (13,845 ft.). Named for the state of Oklahoma, derived from the Choctaw for "red people."

Olathe [ō lā′ thə], town on U.S. 50 in Montrose County (est. 1881, inc. 1907, pop. 1,263). First known as Brown, it was later called Colorow, a name by which the early settlers unwittingly honored a renegade Ute Indian Chief. When this fact became known, the emigrants changed it to Olathe, after a town in Kansas. The word is said to represent a Shawnee (Algonkian) expression meaning "fine, beautiful."

Olney Springs, town on Colorado 96 in Crowley County (est. 1887, inc. 1912, pop. 340). The railroad stop of Olney was apparently named after a representative of the Missouri Pacific Railroad when tracks were laid here. Consecutive stations on the railroad, as one approached Pueblo from the east, were supposedly named alphabetically by the daughter of railroad magnate Jay Gould: thus Arden, Brandon, Chivington . . . Nepesta, Olney, and Pultney.

Olympus, Mount, in Larimer County (8,808 ft.), is named for a mountain in Greece, the mythic home of the ancient gods. **Olympus Heights** is nearby on U.S. 34.

Omega, on U.S. 287 in Larimer County, has the name of the last letter in the Greek alphabet; it also occurs as a woman's given name.

Onahu [on´ ə hōō] **Creek,** in Rocky Mountain National Park, Grand County. Said to be Arapaho for "warms himself," referring to a horse which, on cold evenings, came up to the campfire to get warm.

Ophir [ō´ fər], town in San Miguel County (est. 1878, inc. 1881, pop. 69). For the biblical reference to the location of King Solomon's mines (I Kings 10:11). Similar names are **Ophir Mountain,** in Summit County (10,199 ft.); **Ophir Needles,** in San Miguel County (12,070 ft.); and **Ophir Pass,** also in San Miguel County (11,789 ft.).

Orchard, on Colorado 144 in Morgan County (est. 1890). The present town is about five miles distant from Fremont's Orchard, a once-noted point on an emigrant trail. The "Orchard" was a large grove of stunted cottonwoods which, at a distance, looked like an eastern apple orchard— a welcome sight in staging days across treeless plains. The grove got its name because Colonel John C. Fremont camped here on one of his exploring expeditions. **Orchard City,** a town on Colorado 65 in Delta County (est. 1912, inc. 1912, pop. 2,218), is called the "fruit bowl" of the area. **Orchard Mesa** is a community on U.S. 50 in Mesa County (pop. 5,977). **Orchard Plaza** is in Arapahoe County.

Ordway, town on Colorado 96 (est. 1890, inc. 1900, pop. 1,025); seat of Crowley County. Founded on land taken up by George N. Ordway after he came west after the Civil War.

Ortiz [ōr tēz´], in Conejos County (also pronounced [ōr´ tēz]). Named for its founder, J. Nestor Ortiz.

Osier [ō´ zhər] **Creek,** in Conejos County. An osier is a willow twig used in weaving basketry. Also **Osier Mountain** (10,746 ft.).

Oso [ō′ sō], **Mount,** in La Plata County (13,684 ft.), is from the Spanish word for "bear."

Otero [ō târ′ ō] **County** (area 1,254 sq. mi., pop. 20,185) has La Junta as its seat; it was formed in 1889 out of Bent County. The name was given in honor of Miguel Otero, one of the founders of La Junta, and a member of a prominent Spanish family of southern Colorado and New Mexico. The original meaning of the Spanish surname is "hill." The name Otero was also applied to the town of La Junta on Santa Fe Railroad schedules during 1878. A town called Otero is nearby in New Mexico.

Otis, town on U.S. 34 in Washington County (est. 1883, inc. 1917). For many years it was believed that the name honored Dr. W. O. Otis, an early resident. Later research indicated that Dr. Otis came to Colorado after the town was platted and named. The possibility exists that the town's name may refer to someone connected with the Chicago Burlington and Quincy Railroad. **Otis Peak,** in Rocky Mountain National Park, between Grand and Larimer counties (12,486 ft.), was named for Dr. Edward Osgood Otis of Boston, who climbed in the Estes Park area in the 1880s.

Ouray [o͞o rā′], city on U.S. 550 (est. 1875, inc. 1884, pop. 644); also pronounced [yo͞o rā′]. The city is named for Chief Ouray, a famous leader of the Ute tribe. Present-day Utes offer two explanations of the name. One is that it represents a word *úrí,* meaning "main pole of a tipi" or "king"; in the latter sense, the word may be a loan from Spanish *rey.* The other explanation is that it is from *uur* "arrow." The Chief himself was quoted as saying it was the first word he spoke as a baby. On treaties he signed it "U-Ray" and "U-re." The city was first a silver camp, known as Uncompahgre or Uncompahgre City; it then languished until 1896 when gold was discovered by Thomas F. Walsh, who later became a bonanza king. The city is the seat of, and gives its name to, **Ouray County** (est. 1883, area 540 sq. mi., pop. 1,546), formed from a part of San Juan County. **Mount Ouray** is in Saguache County (13,955 ft.), and **Ouray Peak** in Chaffee County (12,957 ft.).

Ouzel [o͞o zel′] **Peak,** in Rocky Mountain National Park, Boulder County (12,716 ft.); also pronounced [o͞o′ zəl]. Nearby are **Ouzel Creek, Ouzel Falls,** and **Ouzel Lake.** After a bird also called the water ouzel or dipper, *Cinclus mexicanus.*

Ovid [ō′vid], town on U.S. 138 in Sedgwick County (est. 1908, inc. 1925, pop. 349). For many years a siding between Julesburg and Sedgwick, known only to railroad men. The section hands called the location Ovid for Newton Ovid, a bachelor who lived nearby, and the name later became official.

O-Wi-Yu-Kuts [ō wī′ yə kuts] **Plateau,** in Moffat County, supposedly reflects the name of an Indian chief, also spelled Awaiukut. This could perhaps represent Ute *uwáayakach* "they're not coming" or *uwáyakach* "it's not raining."

Owl Creek is the name of five streams in Colorado. **Owl Creek Pass** is between Ouray and Gunnison counties (11,120 ft.). **Owl Mountain** is in Jackson County (10,957 ft.).

Oxford, on Colorado 172, on the Southern Ute Indian Reservation in La Plata County (post office est. 1904). Formerly called Grommet, but supposedly changed to its present name in 1908 "because it sounded better." Separately named is **Mount Oxford,** in Chaffee County (14,153 ft.). This is one of the Collegiate Peaks, but it remained without a name until 1931 when it was named—in keeping with the other college names—by John L. J. Hart.

Pactolus [pak tō′ ləs], in Gilpin County. Named for a river in ancient Asia Minor, famous for its gold-bearing sands.

Padroni [pə drō′ nē], in Logan County (est. 1909). This large sugar beet station was named for two Italian farmers in the vicinity, George and Tom Padroni.

Pagoda, on Colorado 317 in Routt County (est. 1890). Founded by State Senator H. H. Eddy (1887–89), and named for nearby **Pagoda Peak** (11,120 ft.), so called because it resembles an oriental tower. Separately named is **Pagoda Mountain,** in Rocky Mountain National Park, Boulder County (13,497 ft.).

Pagosa [pə gō′ sə] **Springs,** town on U.S. 160 (est. 1883, inc. 1891, pop. 1,207); seat of Archuleta County. The Ute name *pagósa* refers to the sulfurous odor of the springs, which were first seen by whites in July, 1859. **Pagosa Junction** (est. 1899) is in southern Archuleta County. **Pagosa Peak** is to the north, in Mineral County (12,640 ft.).

Pahlone [pä lō′ nē] **Peak,** in Chaffee County (12,667 ft.); also pronounced [pä lōn′]. The name of the son of the Ute leader Chief Ouray. Said by some to mean "short hair"; alternatively, it may represent Ute *parú'ni* "thunder."

Paisaje [pī sä′ hē], in Conejos County, is Spanish for "landscape." The place was originally named San Rafael, and is still called that by local residents. However, it is said that a Protestant resident objected to the name, and had it changed to Paisaje in the early 1900s.

Paiute [pī′ yo͞ot] **Peak,** on the Continental Divide between Grand and Boulder counties. Ellsworth Bethel proposed the name "Ute Peak," since the Utes were the most important tribe in the Colorado Rockies, but the U.S. Board on Geographic Names refused the name, since many other mountains in Colorado bear the same name. Bethel compromised by using the term Paiute, a name for several tribes (in Utah and Nevada) related to the Utes. The word has been said to mean "water Ute" or "true Ute." However, "Ute" is from Spanish *yuta,* whereas "Paiute" is from Spanish *payuchis* (from the native name *payuuchim,* of obscure origin). By false analogy, the English term "Paiute" was made to resemble the tribal name of the Utes.

Palisade, town on U.S. 6 in Mesa County (est. 1895, inc. 1904, pop. 1,871). First called Palisades, for the high perpendicular bluffs which bound the valley on the north.

Palmer Lake, town in El Paso County (est. 1880, inc. 1889, pop. 1,480). Honoring General William J. Palmer of the Denver and Rio Grande Railroad. The lake around which the town is built was christened Palmero by Kate Field, a noted lecturer; but the name was soon changed to Palmer. The town was earlier known as Divide Lake, and the original railroad station was Divide. The post office called it Weissport, for C. A. Weiss, the first railway station agent.

Palo [pal′ ō], meaning "stick, wood, tree" in Spanish, occurs in a number of place names. **Palo Alto** [al′ tō] **Creek,** in Mineral County, refers to a "tall tree." **Palo Duro** [do͞o′ rō] **Creek,** in Huerfano County, refers to "hard wood"; in New Mexican Spanish, *palo duro* refers to the bush called "mountain mahogany" (*Cercocarpus montanus*). **Palos Verdes** [vâr′ dās], in Arapahoe County, means "green trees," referring to the desert shrub *Cercidium floridum,* which has green bark.

Pando [pan´dō], on U.S. 24 in Eagle County. Spanish for "slow of motion, as applied to deep waters"—apparently referring to the nearby Eagle River.

Paoli [pā ō´ lē], on U.S. 6 in Phillips County (est. 1895, inc. 1930, pop. 1,403). Named for Paoli, Pennsylvania, by a chief engineer of the Chicago, Burlington and Quincy Railroad when the line came through here. The Pennsylvania town was named for General Pasquale di Paoli (1725–1807), a Corsican patriot.

Paonia [pā ō´ nē ə], in Delta County (est. 1881, inc. 1902, pop. 1,161); also pronounced [pē ō´ nē ə]. Founded by Samuel Wade, a rancher who established the first general store here. He secured a post office and suggested the name *Paeonia*, the botanical term for the peony. Postal authorities saw fit to change it to Paonia.

Parachute, town on U.S. 6 in Garfield County (est. 1886, inc. 1908, pop. 270). The name of the town was at one time changed to Grand Valley; then, in the 1970s, it was changed back to Parachute, although the post office is still called Grand Valley. When the Colorado town was named, it was said that the forks of **Parachute Creek,** viewed from on high, resembled the shrouds of a parachute.

Paradox, in Montrose County (est. 1882?). The town and the adjacent **Paradox Creek** were named for Paradox Valley, so called because the Dolores River cuts through its cliff walls at right angles. Early settlers found the valley almost inaccessible; they had to unload their wagons, take them apart, and lower the pieces by ropes from a ledge to the floor of the valley.

Parika [pə rē´ kə] **Peak,** in Jackson County (12,394 ft.). From Pawnee *paariíku'* "horn," perhaps because of its shape.

Park County (est. 1861, area 2,162 sq. mi., pop. 7,174). The county seat is Fairplay. Named by the early fur traders and trappers after South Park, one of the four large valleys in the Rockies—the others being North and Middle parks and the San Luis Valley. Park County is one of the original territorial counties.

Parkdale, on U.S. 50 in Fremont County (est. 1878?). Once known as Current Creek Station, it is believed by early settlers to have been named because the Arkansas Valley widens into park-like country here.

Parker, town in Douglas County (est. 1870?, pop. 5,450). In early days this was a station on the stage line from Denver to Colorado Springs. The post office was first called Pine Grove. Later it was changed to Parker, for James S. Parker, who served thirty-three years as postmaster.

Parlin, on U.S. 50 in Gunnison County (est. 1877). Settled by James Parlin, a dairy rancher. Around 1880, officials of the narrow-gauge Denver South Park and Pacific Railroad wanted to buy 1,000 acres of land here for a right-of-way, and asked Parlin his price. The old man in his goodness of heart is said to have replied, "You can have 1,500 acres free if you will put a depot over there by the dairy, and make your trains stop for five minutes." This was to permit the train crew and passengers to drink a glass of milk. Reportedly, the agreement was kept for a time.

Parma, on U.S. 160 and 285 in Rio Grande County. Named for Parma, Idaho, which in turn was named for a city and duchy in Northern Italy. The Colorado name was suggested by Peter Sommers, a rancher of the area.

Parrott City, in La Plata County, was named for Tiburcio Parrott, a San Francisco banker who financed the founder, John Moss. Nearby is **Parrott Peak** (11,857 ft.).

Parshall, on the Colorado River and U.S. 40, in Grand County (est. 1907). Settled by a Mr. Dow, who set up a small store and circulated a petition for a post office. The name Parshall, honoring a pioneer of the region, was suggested.

Patterson, Mount, in Rocky Mountain National Park (11,424 ft.). Named for Senator Thomas M. Patterson, who was influential in establishing the national park.

Pawnee [pô´ nē] is the name of an Indian tribe, once living in the plains of eastern Colorado; the term is now assigned to **Pawnee Buttes,** in Weld County, and to **Pawnee Peak,** one of the Indian Peaks group on the Continental Divide, between Grand and Boulder counties (12,943 ft.). The Pawnee Indians now live in Oklahoma, and call themselves *paári* in their own language; both this and the English term apparently originate in neighboring Siouan languages, e.g. Omaha *ppádhiⁿ*, Oto *páñi*.

Peak to Peak Highway, in Gilpin, Boulder, and Larimer counties, running from Central City to Estes Park. Originally named for its planned route from Estes Park, in the Longs Peak area, to Manitou Springs, near Pikes Peak.

Pearl, in Jackson County, was named in honor of Pearl Burnett, daughter of Benjamin Franklin Burnett. There is a **Pearl Mountain** in Gunnison County (13,362 ft.), and a **Pearl Peak** in Eagle County (12,147 ft.).

Peckham [pek´ əm], on U.S. 85 in Weld County (est. 1898). Orginally a side track on the Union Pacific Railroad, the town came into being when John Peckham opened a cheese factory here.

Peetz, town on Colorado 113 in Logan County (est. 1889, inc. 1917, pop. 179). First named Mercer by the Burlington Railroad when a section house and depot were built here. Because the name was similar to that of a town in western Colorado, the settlement was renamed for Peter Peetz, a pioneer homesteader.

Penrose, community in Fremont County (est. 1908, pop. 2,235). Established by the Beaver Park Land & Water Company, the town was named for Spencer Penrose, a Colorado Springs investor and the company's largest stockholder.

Peterson Field, an air force base in El Paso County. Named for Lieutenant Edward J. Peterson, a native of Colorado, who was killed in an airplane crash at this base in 1942.

Peyton, in El Paso County (est. 1888). Originally called Mayfield, the settlement was renamed in honor of George Peyton, an original settler, after the post office refused to honor the old name.

Phillips County (est. 1889, area 680 sq. mi., pop. 4,189). The county seat is Holyoke. In honor of R. O. Phillips, secretary of the Lincoln Land Company, which organized a number of the towns in eastern Colorado. It was formed from a portion of Logan County.

Phippsburg, on Colorado 131 in Routt County (est. 1905). Established as a division point on the Denver and Salt Lake Railway—being halfway between Kremmling and Steamboat Springs. The name honors U.S. Senator Lawrence C. Phipps, because of his interest in the extension of the railroad.

Piceance [pē´ ans] **Creek** and **Basin,** in Rio Blanco County. Said to be an Indian word for "tall grass." It was first spelled as two words, Pice Ance, but later combined. The discrepancy between the spelling and the pronunciation has not been explained.

Picketwire Valley, in Bent and Las Animas counties. Named for the Purgatoire River, from which the name is taken, but with a distortion of the pronunciation to recall the "picketing" or staking of horses.

Pico [pē′ kō] is a Spanish word for "peak," and occurs at several points in Colorado. **Pico Aislado** [īs lä′ dō], a mountain in Saguache County (13,611 ft.), means "isolated peak."

Pictou [pik′ tōo], in Huerfano County. Named for Pictou, Nova Scotia, Canada, by Tommy Lowther, a mine superintendent who came from there.

Piedra [pē ā′ drə], in Archuleta County, is Spanish for "stone." Nearby is the **Piedra River.** Three mountains in Colorado are called **Piedra Peak;** the highest is in Mineral County (12,328 ft.).

Piedrosa [pē ā drō′ sə] **Creek,** in Conejos County. The word is Spanish for "rocky."

Pierce, town on U.S. 85 in Weld County (est. 1907, inc. 1918, pop. 823). Long before there was a settlement here, the Union Pacific Railroad built a switch and water tank on the site, calling it Pierce after General John Pierce, former Surveyor General of Colorado Territory and one-time president of the Denver Pacific Railroad. When the town was established by John E. and Bert A. Shafer, the name Pierce was retained.

Pikes Peak, in El Paso County (14,110 ft.). Probably one of America's best-known mountains, named for Lieutenant (later General) Zebulon Pike (1779–1813), who first saw it during his expedition of 1806, and called it "Grand Peak." In 1820, during the Long Expedition, it was called James Peak for Edwin James, who was Long's botanist and the first man to climb the mountain. Apparently the final namer was Colonel Henry Dodge, who used the name Pikes Peak on his map of 1835. The name gained prominence during the early Colorado gold rush, when the area became known as Pikes Peak country.

Note that the omission of the apostrophe—"Pikes," not "Pike's"—is in accord with a rule laid down by the U.S. Board on Geographical Names. Also named after Pike are **Pike National Forest,** with headquarters in Park County, and **Pikeview,** a locality in El Paso County.

Pine, in Jefferson County (est. 1882), probably refers to the Ponderosa pine (bull pine, yellow pine, *Pinus ponderosa var. scopulorum*). A post office was established under the name of Pine in 1882. **Pine Creek** is the name of thirteen streams in Colorado. **Pinecliffe,** in Boulder County (est. 1900?), was named by a Dr. Craig, a minister, for an unusually beautiful cliff nearby. The settlement was originally called Gato, Spanish for "cat," in this case perhaps "wildcat." **The Pinery** is a community in Douglas County (pop. 4,885). **Pinewood Springs** is on U.S. 36 in Larimer County (est. 1903?). It was originally called Little Elk Park, but the name was changed about 1960 when a new development was underway.

Pinneo [pi nē′ ō], in Washington County, was named for B. F. Pinneo, a deputy sheriff.

Piñon [pin′ yən], on U.S. 85 and 87 in Pueblo County, is from Spanish *piñón* "pine nut"; also pronounced [pin yōn′]. The name refers to *Pinus edulis,* the pinyon pine, and its delicious seeds. **Piñon Canyon** is a locale in Las Animas County.

Pinos [pē′ nəs] **Creek,** in Rio Grande County, reflects the Spanish for "pine trees." There are also streams called **Los Pinos Creek** in Saguache County, **Los Pinos River** in Hinsdale and La Plata County, and **Rio Pinos** in Conejos County.

Pintada [pin tä′ də] **Mountain,** in Rio Grande County (12,840 ft.). The Spanish word means "painted."

Pinto Creek, in Grand County. The Spanish word means "spotted," and is applied to horses in both Spanish and English.

Pisgah [piz′ gə], **Mount,** is the name of three peaks in Colorado; the highest is in Clear Creek County (10,081 ft.). Named for the mountain east of the Dead Sea from which Moses looked down on the Promised Land just before his death; also called Mount Nebo. The name appears on various heights all over the West, recalling the high hopes of early settlers.

Pitkin [pit′ kin], town in Gunnison County (est. 1879, inc. 1880, pop. 53). First known as Quartzville, but changed to honor Governor Frederick W. Pitkin (1837–86). Independently named is **Pitkin County** (est. 1881, area 973 sq. mi., pop. 12,661), created from a part of Gunnison County. The county seat is Aspen.

Pittsburg, in Gunnison County, is probably named for the Pennsylvania city, which in turn honors William Pitt the Elder, a British statesman (1708–78).

Placerville [plas′ ər vil], on Colorado 145 in San Miguel County (est. 1877?). Founded as a gold-mining town, and named for the placer mines in the vicinity. In 1909 the town was almost completely washed away by a flood. The site was abandoned, and a new depot and business section were built about half a mile up the San Miguel River. The settlement was first referred to as Dry Diggings, and then as Hangtown, prior to its present name.

Placita [plä sē′ tə], on Colorado 133 in Pitkin County. Diminutive of Spanish *plaza,* which in New Mexico and Colorado is used to mean not only a public square, but also a town.

Plateau [plat ō′] **City,** in Mesa County (also pronounced [plat o͞o′]), refers to the topography of the area.

Platoro [plat ōr′ ō], in Conejos County (est. 1882?), is a combination of Spanish *plata* "silver" and *oro* "gold."

Platte [plat] **River,** a major stream of Nebraska, was named in 1739 by the Mallet Brothers, French explorers; because of its shallowness ("a mile wide and an inch deep"), they called it *Rivière Platte,* corresponding to an earlier Spanish name *Río Chato* "flat river" and to the Omaha Indian name *ne braska* "flat water" (whence the English name for the state of Nebraska). Its tributaries, the **North Platte River** and the **South Platte River,** both rise in Colorado.

Platteville, a town on U.S. 85 in Weld County (est. 1871, inc. 1887, pop. 1,515). Founded when the Platte River Land Company purchased several thousand acres in the valleys of the South Platte and St. Vrain rivers.

Plaza, in Rio Grande County, reflects a use of Spanish *plaza,* in New Mexico and Colorado, to mean "town."

Pleasant View, on U.S. 666 in Montezuma County (est. 1941). An earlier settlement, Ackmen, two or three miles to the southwest, was founded around 1913. When the road from Cortez to Dove Creek (now U.S. 666) was made a state highway in the 1930s, a new town was laid out on the newly aligned road, and was called Pleasant View. There is another **Pleasant View** in Jefferson County.

Plum in Colorado place names may refer to the wild plum, *Prunus americana.* **Plum Creek** is a stream in Douglas County, a tributary of the South Platte River. **Plum Valley** is in Las Animas County.

Poncha [pon´ chə] **Mountain,** in Chaffee County (10,134 ft.), and nearby **Poncha Pass,** between Chaffee and Saguache counties (9,010 ft.). Said to be from an unidentified Indian word for "tobacco." At the foot of the pass is **Poncha Springs,** a town on U.S. 50 and 285 in Chaffee County (est. 1879, inc. 1880, pop. 244).

Ponderosa Park, a community in Elbert County (pop. 1,640), is named for *Pinus ponderosa,* a species of pine.

Porphyry [pōr´ fə rē] **Mountain,** in Eagle County (10,856 ft.), is named for a type of hard igneous rock.

Portland, on Colorado 120 in Fremont County, was named for the Portland process of manufacturing cement, developed in Portland, England. Founded as a company town of the Ideal Cement Company. There is also a **Portland** in Ouray County.

Potosi [pō tō´ sē] **Peak,** in Ouray County (13,786 ft.). Named either for San Luis Potosí in Mexico, or for the original Potosí in Bolivia, both famous for their silver mines.

Poudre [pōō´ dər] **Park,** on Colorado 14 in Larimer County (est. 1915). Homesteaded by Thomas H. Farrell, and earlier called Columbine. The name is taken from the adjacent Cache la Poudre River, known locally as the Poudre, from French *poudre* "(gun)powder." This refers to the cache of powder by employees of the American Fur Company who buried supplies—including several kegs of gunpowder—near Laporte, in order to lighten the loads of their teams enroute to the Green River. **Poudre Lake** is in Rocky Mountain National Park, Larimer County.

Powderhorn, in Cebolla Valley, in Gunnison County (est. 1876). This early health resort was originally called White Earth. There are two explanations for the unusual name: One is that Cebolla Valley has the appearance of a huge powderhorn; the other is that a pioneer found a powderhorn on the creek flowing into the Cebolla.

Powell, Lake, in Rocky Mountain National Park, Grand County. Named for John Wesley Powell, leader of the first party to climb Longs Peak in 1868. **Powell Peak,** nearby on the Continental Divide between Grand and Larimer counties (13,208 ft.), was named after the lake. **Mount Powell** is in Summit County (13,560 ft.).

Primero [pri mâr′ ō], in Las Animas County, is Spanish for "first"; it is one of a series of numerically labeled mining operations, opened by the Colorado Fuel and Iron Company in 1904.

Princeton, Mount, in Chaffee County (14,197 ft.). Another in the Collegiate Group, named for Princeton University. It was first known as Chalk Mountain, from Chalk Creek at its base; the present name, used at least since 1873, was probably given by Henry Gannett.

Pritchett, town on U.S. 160 in Baca County (est. 1920, inc. 1923, pop. 153). Marking the western terminus for a branch of the Atchison, Topeka and Santa Fe Railroad, it was named for Dr. Henry S. Pritchett, one of the railroad's directors.

Proctor, on U.S. 138 in Logan County (est. 1908). J. D. Blue, of Cedar Rapids, Iowa, with several friends, purchased five thousand acres here and laid out a townsite along the Union Pacific Railroad. The name was probably given to honor Redfield Proctor, U.S. Secretary of War under President Benjamin Harrison. Other references are to a "General" or "Captain" Proctor, a supposed Indian fighter with General George Crook.

Prospect Valley, on Colorado 52 and 79 in Weld County (est. 1922); the community was established by John G. Michael.

Prowers [prou′ ərz] **County** (est. 1889, area 1,621 sq. mi., pop. 13,347). The county seat is Lamar. Named for John W. Prowers (1838–84), the pioneer who introduced the first Hereford cattle to the Arkansas Valley, driving the herd from Missouri. The county was once part of Bent County.

Pryor, in Huerfano County (est. 1867). For Mack and Ike Pryor, who settled here just after the Civil War and went into the cattle business.

Ptarmigan [tär′ mi gən] **Pass,** on the Continental Divide between Grand and Larimer counties (11,777 ft.), is named for the white-tailed ptarmigan, a bird resembling a grouse (*Lagopus leucurus*). Nearby **Ptarmigan Creek, Lake,** and **Point** (12,363 ft.) are named for the pass. **Ptarmigan Mountain,** some distance away in Grand County (12,324 ft.), was named independently. Three mountains in Colorado are called **Ptarmigan Peak;** the highest is in Lake County (13,739 ft.).

Pueblo [pweb′ lō], city on U.S. 50, 85, and 87 (est. 1858, inc. 1885, pop. 98,640). Old-fashioned pronunciations are [peb′ lō, pē yeb′ lō, pyōo eb′ lō]. Originally called Independence, after the town in Missouri. However, the settlement was soon renamed Pueblo, Spanish for "town" or "village." Pueblo had been a settlement for many years before, being occupied at intervals by Spaniards, trappers, Indian traders, and Mexicans. In 1806 Lieutenant Zebulon Pike erected a crude log cabin here, and Major Jacob Fowler, a trapper, built a log house here in 1822. By 1841 there was even an adobe fort. The city is the seat of, and gave its name to, **Pueblo County** (est. 1861, area 2,405 sq. mi., pop. 123,051). It is one of the seventeen original territorial counties.

Puma [pōō′ mə] **Hills,** in Park County, is named after *Felis concolor,* the native cat also known as the mountain lion, cougar, or panther. The Spanish word *puma* is itself borrowed from the Quechua language of Peru.

Punche [pōōn′ chē] **Valley,** in Conejos County; also known as El Punche. Probably a Spanish adaptation of a Ute name, perhaps the same as that reflected in Poncha Pass.

Punkin Center, on Colorado 71 and 94 in Lincoln County (est. 1918?). Earlier called Prairie Dream. The name is a corruption of "pumpkin," because of large pumpkins grown in the area.

Purcell, in Weld County (est. 1910), honors Lawrence M. Purcell, upon whose land the town was located. An earlier stub line and station of the Union Pacific Railroad was called Hungerford, for the superintendent of the Pullman Car Company.

Purgatoire [pûr gə twär′] **River,** in Las Animas and Bent counties. From the French word for "purgatory," translating the earlier Spanish name *Río de las Ánimas Perdidas en Purgatorio* "River of the Lost Souls in Purgatory." An English corruption of the French name is reflected in the place name "Picketwire Valley." **Purgatoire Peak** is in Costilla County (13,676 ft.). Separately named is **Purgatory Creek,** in La Plata County.

Pyramid Peak, in Pitkin County (14,018 ft.), is named for its shape.

Quandary [kwän′ drē] **Peak,** in Summit County (14,265 ft.). So named because prospectors in the early 1860s were puzzled at strange outcroppings of silver ore in the area.

Querida [kə rē′ də], in Custer County, is Spanish for "beloved, darling."

Rabbit **Creek** is the name of three streams in Colorado. **Rabbit Ears Peak,** in Jackson County (10,654 ft.), is named for its double projecting shape; the peak gives its name to nearby **Rabbit Ears Pass,** on the Continental Divide, between Grand and Jackson counties (9,426 ft.).

Radium, in Grand County (post office est. 1906). The name was suggested by Harry S. Porter, prospector and miner, in 1906, because of the radium content in a mine he owned near the town.

Ragged Peak, in Gunnison County (12,641 ft.); part of the **Ragged Mountains,** also called the **Raggeds.** The mountains were named for their jagged appearance by a man named Wood, an early prospector; Woods Lake northeast of Marble is named for him. Ragged Mountain Post Office, on East Muddy Creek, was opened in 1919.

Rainbow Creek is the name of only two streams in Colorado, but there are sixteen bodies of water called **Rainbow Lake. Rainbow Bay** is in Lake Granby, Rocky Mountain National Park, Grand County; it is named for the rainbow trout, introduced from the West Coast, which now make up a large portion of the trout caught in Colorado. **Rainbow Valley** is a locale in Teller County.

Rajadero [rä hä dâr′ ō] **Canyon,** in Conejos County, is from Spanish *rajadero* "place of splitting" (e.g., splitting wood), from *rajar* "to split."

Ramah [rā′ mə], town on U.S. 24 in El Paso County (est. 1888, inc. 1927, pop. 94). The name was given by the El Paso Land & Water Company, which platted the town. In the Bible, Ramah is one of the cities of the allotment of Benjamin; it is said to mean "hill."

Ramsey Peak, in the Mummy Range, Rocky Mountain National Park (11,582 ft.). Named for Hugh Ramsey, who homesteaded in the area in 1890.

Rams Horn Mountain, Rocky Mountain National Park, Larimer County, near Estes Park (9,314 ft.). Earlier called Sheep Mountain because of the abundant bighorn sheep.

Rand, on Colorado 125 in Jackson County (est. 1881?). Named for a frontier scout and early pioneer, Jack Rand. A post office was established in 1883.

Rangely [rānj′ lē], town on Colorado 64 in Rio Blanco County (est. 1885, inc. 1946, pop. 2,278). Settled as a trading post by Charles and Frank Hill and D. B. Case. Case named the settlement for Rangeley, Maine, the former home of Charles Hill.

Raton [rə tōn´] **Pass,** on U.S. 85 and 87 between Colorado and New Mexico. An old-fashioned pronunciation is [rə tōōn´]. From Spanish *ratón* "mouse," also used in New Mexico and Colorado to mean "squirrel."

Rattlesnake, referring to the poisonous serpent, gives its name to **Rattlesnake Buttes,** in Huerfano County. Three streams in the state are called **Rattlesnake Creek.**

Rawah [rā´ wə] **Peaks,** in Larimer County, includes North Rawah Peak (12,473 ft.) and South Rawah Peak (12,644 ft.). Perhaps from Ute *urá'wa* "crest of a mountain ridge."

Raymer, town on Colorado 14 in Weld County (est. 1888, inc. 1919, pop. 98). Most of the district was vacated in 1893 to 1894, but the site was again platted in 1909. The Lincoln Land Company named the town after George Raymer, an assistant chief engineer on the Burlington and Missouri Railroad. The post office is called New Raymer to avoid confusion with the town of Ramah, in El Paso County.

Raymond, on Colorado 72 in Boulder County (est. 1895?). Previously called Raymond Ranch, for local settlers, and later Raymonds (with no apostrophe).

Red is a term which forms part of many Colorado place names, often referring to red rocks or earth. **Red Cliff** is a town in Eagle County (est. 1879, inc. 1880, pop. 297), previously called simply Cliff.

Redcloud Peak, in Hinsdale County (14,034 ft.), was named for its ruddy coloration, and because the upper ridges were thought to resemble clouds. First called Red Mountain, it was named Red Cloud by the Hayden Survey in 1874.

Red Creek is the name of eight streams in the state. **Red Feather Lakes,** in Larimer County (est. 1923), was founded by Mr. Princell and named by him for Chief Redfeather, hero of a Cherokee Indian legend.

Red Hill is the name of eight summits in the state; the highest is in Jackson County (10,679 ft.). **Red Hill Pass** is in Park County (9,993 ft.).

Red Lion, in Logan County, was named after the Red Lion flour mill, owned by E. O. Wright.

Redmesa, on the Southern Ute Indian Reservation, on Colorado 140 in La Plata County (est. 1908). It was founded by Mormon settlers and first called Garland, but the name was unsatisfactory because of another Garland in the state. At a group meeting, the settlers chose the new name Red Mesa.

Red Mountain is the name of fourteen peaks in the state; the highest is in Costilla County (13,908 ft.). The settlement of **Red Mountain** is on U.S. 550 in Ouray County (est. 1882?). Nearby is **Red Mountain Pass,** between Ouray and San Juan counties (11,018 ft.).

Red Rock is the name of twenty features in the state. **Red Rock Amphitheater,** in Jefferson County, is a natural site, named for the surrounding sandstone monoliths, four hundred feet high.

Redstone, on Colorado 133 in Pitkin County (est. 1903). Named for the vivid red rocks nearby when founded by the Colorado Fuel & Iron Company as a model industrial village.

Redvale, on Colorado 145 in Montrose County (est. 1908?). Originally called Redlands because of the reddish soil in the area. With the coming of the post office, the name was changed to Redvale to avoid confusion with Redlands, California.

Red Wing, in Huerfano County (est. 1913). When the first store was built here, residents asked for a post office and requested the name Crestone. This was refused because of a town by that name in Saguache County. As a group of residents discussed the rejection, a man came by whistling the tune "Red Wing"; the name was sent to the post office and approved.

Republican Mountain, in Clear Creek County (12,386 ft.), was probably named by political partisans. Independently named is the **Republican River,** the South Fork of which runs from Lincoln County, through Kit Carson and Yuma counties, and on into Kansas. The name is associated with the so-called "Republican" or Kitkehatki band of the Pawnee Indian tribe.

Resolis [rə zō′ ləs], in Elbert County, was platted in 1888. The name may be from Spanish *resoles,* translatable as "reflections of the sun's rays."

Rezago [rə zä′ gō], in Las Animas County, may reflect a Spanish word meaning "remainder, residue."

Rhyolite [rī′ ō līt] **Mountain,** in Teller County (10,780 ft.). The name refers to an igneous rock, rich in silica.

Richthofen [rikt′ hō fən], **Mount,** part of the Never Summer Mountains, in Rocky Mountain National Park, Grand County (12,940 ft.). Named sometime before 1876 for Baron Ferdinand von Richthofen, a nineteenth-century German geologist—not for Baron Walter von Richthofen, a German businessman who came to Denver in 1877, and who was the uncle of Manfred von Richthofen, the German flying ace of World War I.

Rico [rē′ kō], town on Colorado 145 in Dolores County (est. 1879, inc. 1880, pop. 92); formerly the county seat. After Colonel J. C. Haggerty's discovery of silver in 1879, a rush of prospectors poured into the district. After the settlement had been called Carbon City, Carbonville, Lead City, and Dolores City, a meeting was finally called to choose a new name. William Weston, then of Ouray, suggested the Spanish word *rico* "rich," which was adopted.

Ridgway, town on Colorado 62 in Ouray County (est. 1890, inc. 1891, pop. 423). Named for R. M. Ridgway, superintendent of the Mountain Division of the Denver and Rio Grande Railroad.

Rifle, city on U.S. 6 in Garfield County (est. 1882, inc. 1905, pop. 4,636), is named for **Rifle Creek.** About 1880, several soldiers were working on the road between Meeker and the present site of Rifle, placing mileposts between the Colorado and White rivers. One of the men left his rifle at a night camp. When he discovered his loss, he returned for it and found it on the bank of a stream, which was immediately named Rifle Creek.

Riland [rī′ lənd], in Garfield County, was named for "Dad" Riland, first settler in this vicinity.

Rio [rē′ ō], Spanish for "river," occurs in the names of many Colorado streams, and of other geographical features named after those streams. Thus **Rio Blanco** [bläng′ kō] is a locale on Colorado 13 in Rio Blanco County (est. 1899), also written Rioblanco; this is from Spanish *Río Blanco* "White River"—now the English name of the river. But the town of Rio Blanco is on what is now called Piceance Creek, a tributary of the White River. Also named for that river is **Rio Blanco County** (est. 1889, area 3,263 sq. mi., pop. 5, 972). The county seat is not Rio Blanco, but Meeker. The county was formed from a part of Garfield County.

Rio Grande [rē′ ō grand′], a river which rises in San Juan County and flows through southeastern Colorado into New Mexico, and then forms the boundary between Texas and Mexico. Since the name is from Spanish *Río Grande (del Norte)* "Great River (of the North)," it is considered redundant to say "Rio Grande River" in English. Alternative pronunciations are [rē′ ə grand′, rē′ ō gran′ dē]; an old-fashioned pronunciation is [rī′ ō grand′]. The name currently used in Mexico is *Río Bravo (del Norte)* "Wild River (of the North)." **Rio Grande County** (est. 1874, area 915 sq. mi., pop. 10,770) is named for the river; the county seat is Del Norte. Created from a portion of Conejos County. **Rio Grande Pyramid** (13,821 ft.) in Hinsdale County is a prominent San Juan landmark.

Rio Pinos [rē′ ō pē′ nōs] is in Conejo County; in Spanish, it means "river (of) pines."

Rito [rē′ tō] is a term meaning "creek" in the Spanish of New Mexico and Colorado; it is the diminutive of *río* "river." **Rito Alto** [al′ tō] thus means "high creek"; it appears in the redundant name **Rito Alto Creek,** in Saguache County, and is also given to the nearby **Rito Alto Peak** (13,794 ft.). **Rito Gato** [gä′ tō], a stream in Conejos County, means "cat creek." **Rito Hondo** [hon′ dō], in Hinsdale County, means "deep creek." **Rito Oso** [ō′ sō], in Huerfano County, means "bear creek." **Rito Seco** [sā′ kō], referring to streams in both Costilla and Las Animas counties, means "dry creek."

River Bend, on U.S. 40 and 287 in Elbert County (est. 1870). One of the older settlements in eastern Colorado, on Big Sandy Creek, upon whose banks the Sand Creek Massacre of 1864 occurred. The town's name comes from its location on a bend in Big Sandy Creek.

Roaring Fork River, a tributary of the Colorado River, is named for its turbulence; it rises in Pitkin County, flowing through Eagle and Garfield counties. There is also a **Roaring Fork** of the North Platte River, in Jackson County.

Rock Creek is the name of twenty-two streams in Colorado. **Rock Mountain** is in Hinsdale County (10,182 ft.).

Rockport, on U.S. 85 in Weld County (est. 1926). Built on land owned by Clark Coleman, named by him for Rockport, Illinois. However, the first building was of rocks gathered in the area.

Rockvale, town in Fremont County (est. 1882, inc. 1886, pop. 321). The Santa Fe Railway proposed that a settlement be named for the former owner of the land, B. F. Rockafellow; but he preferred that it be named for Rockvale, Maryland, which he said was "a beautiful valley bound in by rocky walls." Rockafellow's regiment had camped there during the Civil War.

Rocky Flats, on Colorado 93 in Jefferson County, is named for the stony terrain. It is the site of a plant of the U.S. Atomic Energy Commision.

Rocky Ford, on U.S. 50 in Otero County (est. 1870, inc. 1887, pop. 4,162). Two towns of this name were founded. The first was on the Arkansas River, twenty miles above Bent's Fort, at a ford used in time of high water by freighters and cattle drives. A post office was established and a small settlement grew. When the Santa Fe Railway was extended to Pueblo, the post office and store moved from the old town to the site of the present city, about three miles to the southwest. The name comes from the gravel-lined ford across the river.

Rocky Mountains, the principal range in Colorado, were named with a translation of French *Montagnes Rocheuses*, first applied to the Canadian Rockies. Apparently French Canadians first applied the name not because the mountains were rocky (most mountains are), but rather with reference to the "Rock" or Assiniboin Indian tribe, a Siouan subgroup. These Indians were called *assinii-pwaan*, literally "Stone Sioux," by their Cree (Algonkian) neighbors. The Rocky Mountains have given their name to many other features in Colorado. **Rocky Mountain Arsenal,** in Adams County, was established in 1942 to manufacture and store chemical weapons. It is now closed, and off limits to the public because of toxic pollution, but is used as a wildlife preserve. **Rocky Mountain National Park** is in Larimer and Grand counties. The original plan was to call it Estes National Park. However, there was a plan to include several other areas in the national park, including Mount Evans and Pikes Peak; and in 1915, when the park was established, the name was changed to allow for these possibilities.

Roggen [rog´ ən], on U.S. 6 in Weld County (est. 1883?), was first known as Blair, but was changed by the postal authorities because of confusion with Blair, Nebraska. The name Roggen was given by postal authorities. One version is that it was named for one of the surveyors of the

Burlington and Missouri Railroad. Another version is that the name honors Edward P. Roggin, a former Nebraska Secretary of State.

Rollinsville, on Colorado 119 in Gilpin County (est. 1861?). Founded by John Q. A. Rollins, an early cattle rancher. The early mining camp was unique in that saloons, gambling houses, and dance halls were not allowed. The settlement was the starting point of a wagon road constructed by Rollins over the Continental Divide—called **Rollins Pass,** where Boulder, Gilpin, and Grand counties come together (11,670 ft.)— and on into Hot Sulphur Springs and Middle Park.

Romeo [rō´ mē ō], town on U.S. 285 and Colorado 142 in Conejos County (est. 1899, inc. 1923, pop. 341). Some sources say that the name was originally Romero, a Spanish surname; however, the post office was called Romeo when it first opened in 1901.

Roosevelt [roo͞´ sə velt] **National Forest,** in Larimer and Boulder counties. Earlier called Colorado National Forest; changed in 1932 in honor of President Theodore Roosevelt, who established it.

Rosa, Mount, in Teller County (11,499 ft.). Named for Rose Kingsley, an English writer who first visited the area in 1871 to 1872; she used the pen name *Rosa del Monte,* literally "mountain rose."

Rosedale, in Weld County (est. 1939, inc. 1939). Platted as a forty-acre settlement on Greeley's south border to circumvent "dry" laws of that city. (Greeley was a "temperance" town until 1969.) At one time the nickname "Boozeville" was applied. The original plat was filed by George E. Kendrick and his wife, Rose Agnes Kendrick. The name would seem to stem from her first name.

Rosemont, in Teller County, is named for nearby Mount Rosa.

Rosita [rō zē´ tə], in Custer County (est. 1870). Richard Irwin, prospector and writer, established a camp here which developed into a settlement which became known as Rosita (Spanish for "little rose").

Roswell, in El Paso County, was named for Roswell P. Flower of New York City.

Roubideau [roo͞´ bi dō], in Delta County, was named for Antoine Roubideau, a French trader from St. Louis, Missouri, who constructed Fort Uncompahgre near Delta in 1837. The name is also spelled Robideau, Robidoux, and Roubidoux.

Round Mountain is the name of eleven peaks in Colorado. The highest is in Saguache County (12,912 ft.).

Routt [rout] **County** (est. 1877, area 2,330 sq. mi., pop. 14,088). The county seat is Steamboat Springs. In honor of John L. Routt (1826–1907), last territorial and first state governor of Colorado. It was at Steamboat Springs that the Norwegian Karl Howelson demonstrated the art of ski-jumping, thereby causing this and other areas of Colorado to become important places for skiing. The county was formed from part of Grand County.

Rowe [rou] **Glacier,** in the Mummy Range, Rocky Mountain National Park; also **Rowe Peak** (13,400 ft.) and **Rowe Mountain** (13,184 ft.). The glacier was formerly called Hallett Glacier, but was renamed in 1932 for Israel Rowe, the pioneer who discovered it.

Rowena [rō ē′ nə], in Boulder County. The post office was opened 1894, and closed in 1918. The woman's name Rowena became popular as the name of an Anglo-Saxon princess, the heroine of Sir Walter Scott's novel *Ivanhoe.*

Roxborough [roks′ bə rō] **State Park,** in Douglas County. Named by an Britisher, Edward McKenzie Griffith, presumably after the historic county in Scotland (also spelled Roxburgh).

Royal Gorge, a locale in Fremont County (est. 1929), was named for the Royal Gorge of the Arkansas River. By congressional action, in 1906 a two-thousand-acre park was created along the rim of the spectacular gorge. In 1929 a suspension bridge was constructed across the gorge. A post office was opened in 1949.

Ruby Canyon, in Mesa County, on the Colorado River. Probably named for "ruby silver," a type of silver ore. **Ruby Mountain** is the name of three peaks in the state; the highest is in Summit County (13,277 ft.).

Rugby, in Las Animas County. Supposedly named for Rugby, England, by an Englishman who owned mines in the vicinity.

Rulison [rōō′ lə sən], on U.S. 6 in Garfield County, was named after C. M. Rulison.

Rush, on Colorado 94 in El Paso County (est. 1907), was named for Christopher Rush, a homesteader who came from Missouri and settled here in 1907.

Russell, on U.S. 160 in Costilla County, was named for W. Green Russell, who discovered gold in Gray Back Gulch. It was earlier called Placer. Also named for W. Green Russell is **Russell Gulch** in Gilpin County.

Rustic, on Colorado 14 in Larimer County (est. 1882), was established with the Rustic Hotel built by S. B. Stewart at the foot of Pingree Hill. Presidents Ulysses S. Grant and Theodore Roosevelt are said to have vacationed there.

Ruxton, on Colorado 94 in El Paso County, was named for George Ruxton, an English hunter who visited the area in 1847 to 1848.

Rye, town on Colorado 165 in Pueblo County (est. 1882, inc. 1937, pop. 168), was named for the grain which surrounded the town. The first post office was established at the ranch of David Nichols, and was known as Table Mountain. Because postal authorities objected to the lengthy name, it was changed to Rye sometime before 1885.

Ryssby [ris´ bē], in Boulder County (est. 1869), was founded by settlers from the town of Ryssby in Småland province, Sweden. The name refers to a clearing in a forest.

Saguache [sə wäch´], town on U.S. 285 (est. 1867, inc. 1891, pop. 584). From Ute *sagwách,* referring to the color range that includes both green and blue. Some present-day Ute speakers believe the place name refers to green vegetation; others believe it refers to bluish stones or earth. A different spelling is used in the name of the Sawatch Range, in Gunnison, Chaffee, and Saguache counties. The city is the seat of, and gives its name to, **Saguache County** (est. 1867, area 3,144 sq. mi., pop. 4,619), originally formed from part of Costilla County.

Saint Elmo [sānt el´ mō], in Chaffee County (est. 1880). Originally named Forest City because it was necessary to cut down a heavy growth of pine and spruce trees before the town could be built. However, postal authorities refused the name because of a conflict with a Forest City in California. Griffith Evans, first store operator, had recently read the sentimental novel *Saint Elmo,* by Augusta Jane Evans, and suggested the title for the town.

Saint Vrains, in Weld County, for Ceran Saint Vrain, who in the 1830s was associated with the Bent Brothers in trading enterprises. Also named for him, in Boulder County, are **Saint Vrain Creek** and **Saint Vrain Mountain** (12,162 ft.). The family name Saint Vrain derives from a place name in France, which in turn comes from the name of Saint Veranus, bishop of Cavaillon (died A.D. 589).

Salida [sə lī′ də], city on U.S. 50 (est. 1880, inc. 1891, pop. 4,737); seat of Chaffee County. Spanish for "outlet," referring to the place where the Arkansas Valley opens out. The town was founded by the Denver and Rio Grande Railway when it reached here in 1880, and was named South Arkansas. The post office ordered the name changed in 1881, on a suggestion from Governor Alexander C. Hunt, an official of the railroad, who had recently visited Mexico.

Salina [sə lī′ nə], in Boulder County. Named for Salina, Kansas. The word is Spanish for "salt pan."

Sams, on Colorado 62 in San Miguel County, was named for an early day saw mill operator.

San, Spanish for "saint," occurs in many Colorado place names; the feminine form is Santa, but this has sometimes been changed by English speakers, as in "San Isabel." **San Acacio** [ə kash′ ē ō], on Colorado 142 in Costilla County (est. 1853), is also pronounced [ə kas′ ē ō]; it was named for Saint Acacius, a Spanish soldier who was canonized—not "cannonized," as stated in one source. The first Spanish settlers here fought Indians in the name of San Acacio, and later named their post office for him.

San Antonio, in Conejos County, is Spanish for "Saint Anthony." **San Arroyo** [ə roi′ yō] **Creek,** in Adams County, meaning literally "saint creek creek," may represent a garbled form of some saint's name; the alternative form Santa Arroyo Creek, with the feminine form for "saint," makes even less sense. **San Cristobal** [kris tō′ bəl] **Lake,** in Hinsdale County, reflects Spanish *San Cristóbal* "Saint Christopher."

Sand Creek is the name of twenty-three streams in Colorado, and four others are called **Sandy Creek.** Near one of these, **Big Sandy Creek** in Kiowa County, a party of Arapaho and Cheyenne Indians was slaughtered in 1864 by Colorado troops under Colonel John M. Chivington. The incident is known as the Sand Creek Massacre.

Sanford, town on Colorado 136 in Conejos County (est. 1881?, inc. 1907, pop. 750). Founded as a Mormon settlement and originally given the biblical name of Ephraim, the younger son of Joseph. Later it was renamed to honor Silas Sanford Smith, first president of the San Luis Stake.

San Francisco, in Costilla County (est. 1854), is Spanish for "Saint Francis," but was probably named in honor of Colonel John Francisco.

Sangre de Cristo [sang′ grē dē kris′ tō] **Pass,** in Costilla County (9,468 ft.). Named for the **Sangre de Cristo Range,** in Saguache, Fremont, and Custer counties. The Spanish phrase meaning "Blood of Christ" was applied because of the red glow of the winter snow cover when struck by the sun.

San Isabel [iz′ ə bel], on Colorado 165 in Custer County. Named for **San Isabel Creek,** in Saguache County: a garbled form of Spanish *Santa Isabel* "Saint Elizabeth."

Sanitas [san′ i təs] **Mountain,** in Boulder County (ca. 6,600 ft.); also pronounced [sə nē′ təs]. Latin for "health"; the name was inspired by the old Boulder Sanitarium, now the Mapleton Rehabilitation Center.

San Juan [hwän′], in Las Animas County; also pronounced [wän′]. Spanish for "Saint John." Separately named is **San Juan County** (est. 1876, area 391 sq. mi., pop. 745); the county seat is Silverton. The name was given by the Dominguez-Escalante expedition of 1776 to the **San Juan River** (now in Archuleta County), a tributary of the Navajo River; it was later extended to the **San Juan Mountains** (Archuleta and Conejos counties), and subsequently to the general region and to this county. Another San Juan River flows through the southwest corner of Montezuma County before joining the Colorado River in Utah.

San Luis [loo′ is], town on Colorado 159 (est. 1851, inc. 1968, pop. 800); seat of Costilla County. Spanish for "Saint Louis"; the pronunciation [loo′ ē] is sometimes heard, especially in the expression **San Luis Valley.** A pronunciation closer to Spanish is [sän loo ēs′]. The town is called the oldest in Colorado, the original site being three-fourths of a mile below the present one. It was on the Sangre de Cristo Land Grant, given to Luis Lee and Narciso Beaubien in December 1843. For many years it was known as Culebra or San Luis de Culebra, and as Plaza del Medio "center village," while San Pedro, three miles above, was called Upper Culebra or Plaza Arriba, and San Acacio, three miles below, was Lower Culebra or Plaza Abajo. Named from the same source is **San Luis Peak,** in Saguache County (14,014 ft.).

San Miguel [mi gil´] is on Colorado 145 in **San Miguel County** (est. 1883, area 1,283 sq. mi., pop. 3,653). The county seat is Telluride. The name, Spanish for "St. Michael," was first given to the **San Miguel River** (San Miguel and Montrose counties), and later to the county, formed from a portion of Ouray County. There is also a San Miguel in Las Animas County.

San Pablo [pab´ lō], in Costilla County (est. 1851). Spanish for "Saint Paul." Named along with the adjacent community of **San Pedro** [pā´ drō] "St. Peter."

Santa Fe [san tə fā´], a postal station in Denver, is Spanish for "holy faith."

Santa Maria [mə rē´ ə], on U.S. 285 and the South Platte River, in Park County. Spanish for "Saint Mary."

Sapinero [sap i när´ ō], on U.S. 50 in Gunnison County (est. 1888). Named in honor of Sapinero, a sub-chief of the Ute Indians, and a brother-in-law of Chief Ouray.

Sarcillo [sär sē´ ō], a locale in Las Animas County. For *zarcillo,* which in the Spanish of New Mexico and Colorado refers to a plant called "bleeding heart."

Sargents, on U.S. 50 in Saguache County (est. 1879?). Named for Joseph Sargent, once connected with the Los Pinos Indian Agency, who established a ranch here in 1879. In 1880 the ranch became a town, and a post office was named Marshalltown, with Joseph Sargent as postmaster. The name of the settlement was changed to Sargents in 1882.

Sarruche [sə rōō´ chē] **Canyon,** in Las Animas County, is probably for Spanish *serruche,* which means "handsaw" in the dialect of New Mexico and Colorado.

Satank [sə tank´], in Garfield County (post office est. 1886), is named for a Kiowa chief better known as Satanta (*sei´-täiⁿ-dei* "white bear"). **Santanta Peak,** in Grand County (11,979 ft.), is probably another version of the same name.

Saugus [sô′ gəs], on U.S. 24, in Lincoln County (post office est. 1908), was probably named after Saugus, Massachusetts. The Algonkian name means "small outlet."

Sawatch [sə wäch′] **Range,** in Gunnison, Chaffee, and Saguache counties; a different spelling of the name Saguache.

Sawpit, town on Colorado 145 in San Miguel County (est. 1895?, inc. 1896, pop. 36). A saw pit was a pit in the ground used by a two-man crew to saw lumber. A log was placed over the pit, and two men worked a huge saw—one man above, and the other below.

Schramm, on U.S. 34 in Yuma County. Named for Raimond von Harrom Schramm, a wealthy German of noble lineage who came here from New York in 1888. Acquiring considerable property in the city of Yuma, he told people there that, unless they elected him mayor, he would move all his possessions to his own town of Schramm. He won the election.

Security-Widefield, on U.S. 85 and 87 in El Paso County (est. 1955). The twin community has a population of 23,822. Security was established as a new community by American Builders, with a name designed to convey reassurance to buyers. In 1968 Jules Watson started a development called Widefield Homes, expressing the concept of open space.

Sedalia [si dāl′ yə], on U.S. 85 in Douglas County (est. 1865). John H. Craig, who settled in Happy Canon in 1859, founded the present town of Sedalia as the Round Corral in 1865. In 1870 it was sold and became Plum Station or the Town of Plum, named after East and West Plum creeks. Later one of the original settlers, a native of Sedalia, Missouri, changed the name to its present one.

Sedgwick, on the South Platte River and highway 138 (est. 1887, inc. 1918, pop. 208). Named for historic Fort Sedgwick (1864–71), a few miles east of the town. The fort in turn was named in 1865 to honor Major General John Sedgwick, who led Indian campaigns in Colorado in 1857 and 1860, but was killed in the Civil War in 1864. Also named for him is **Sedgwick County** (est. 1889, area 544 sq. mi., pop. 2,690), of which the seat is Julesburg. The county was created in the extreme northeast corner of the state from part of Logan County.

Sego [sē′ gō] **Springs,** in Conejos County, is probably named after the sego lily or mariposa lily, *Calochortus gunnisonii* (the state flower of Utah). The name is from Southern Paiute *sigó'*.

Segundo [si gun′ dō], in Las Animas County (est. 1901?). When the Colorado Fuel & Iron Company bought large holdings in this region and began coal production, it named each coal mine and camp by number as it was opened. Segundo, Spanish for "second," was the second camp founded.

Seibert [sī′ bərt], town on U.S. 24 in Kit Carson County (est. 1888, inc. 1917, pop. 181); also pronounced [sē′ bərt]. For Henry Seibert, New York millionaire and an official of the Rock Island Railroad when the line came through here in 1888.

Severance, in Weld County (est. 1910, inc. 1920, pop. 106). For Dave Severance, who sold 160 acres of land to the Denver-Larimer Townsite Company, at a then astronomical price of $325 an acre.

Shaffers [shā′ fərz] **Crossing,** on U.S. 285 in Jefferson County (est. 1865?). For pioneer settler Samuel Shaffer, on whose land the community started.

Shavano [shav′ ə nō], a locale in Chaffee County, named for nearby **Mount Shavano** (14,229 ft.). The mountain was in turn named for Shavano, a chief of the Tabeguache Band of the Ute tribe, who was a signer of a treaty with the United States in 1873; his name appears on the document as "Chavanaux." The name may have been applied to the chief by a white, since it seems to reflect a native term for the Shawnee, an Algonkian tribe of the Ohio Valley; its literal meaning is "southerner."

Shaw, in Lincoln County, is named for Charles Shaw, who came here from Iowa in 1908.

Shawnee [shô′ nē], on U.S. 285 in Park County (est. 1878?). Named for nearby **Shawnee Peak** (12,400 ft.) by the Denver South Park and Pacific Railroad in 1880. The name honors the Shawnee Indian tribe. It is derived from *shawun* "southerly," the tribe's correct name being *Shawunogi* "southerners." Originally the tribe came from South Carolina and Tennessee.

Sheep Creek is the name of fifteen streams in Colorado. There are nineteen peaks called **Sheep Mountain;** the highest is in San Juan County (13,292 ft.). The term is likely to refer to the wild mountain sheep. **Sheephorn** is in Eagle County.

Sheridan, city on U.S. 285 in Arapahoe County (est. 1887, inc. 1890, pop. 4,976). Originally called Petersburg, in honor of Peter Magnes, "the father of the sugar beet industry." Later renamed for General Philip Sheridan (1831–88) of Civil War fame; the incorporation included the settlements of Sheridan Park, Military Park, Logantown, and Petersburg. **Sheridan Lake,** a town on Colorado 96 in Kiowa County (est. 1887, inc. 1951, pop. 95), is named after an adjacent lake which also honors General Sheridan. **Mount Sheridan,** in Lake and Park counties (13,748 ft.), was named for the general by the Hayden exploring party around 1872.

Sherman, Mount, in Lake and Park counties (14,036 ft.). Named by the Hayden party around 1872, for Civil War General William T. Sherman (1820–91).

Shoshone [shə shōn´], on U.S. 6 in Garfield County. Named for an Indian tribe, also called Shoshoni, close relatives to the Ute tribe of Colorado. Their original territories and their present day residences are in Nevada, Utah, Idaho, and Wyoming. **Shoshoni Peak** is one of the Indian Peaks group, in Grand County (12,967 ft.).

Sierra [sē âr´ ə], in Costilla County, is Spanish for "mountain range." **Sierra Vista,** in Pueblo County, is mock-Spanish for "mountain view"; more correct would be *Vista de la Sierra.*

Silex, Mount, in San Juan County (13,628 ft.), reflects the Latin word for "flint."

Siloam [sī´ lō əm], on U.S. 6 in Pueblo County. Named for the healing pool of water made famous by the biblical story of the blind man (John, 9). Said to mean "sent" in Hebrew.

Silt, on U.S. 6 in Garfield County (est. 1908, inc. 1915, pop. 1,095). Founded by Henry Halsey, townsite owner, and originally called Ferguson. The settlement was renamed by the Denver and Rio Grande Western Railroad because of the nature of the soil.

Silver Creek is the name of eighteen streams in Colorado. Six peaks are called **Silver Mountain;** the highest is in Huerfano County (13,714 ft.). **Silver Cliff** is a town on Colorado 96 in Custer County (est. 1878, inc. 1879, pop. 322). In 1877 silver deposits were discovered here, and soon rich mines were established. As miners rushed into the area, the growing town (which once aspired to be the state capital) took the name Silver Cliff.

Silverheels, Mount, in Park County (13,817 ft.), supposedly named for a dancing girl who wore shoes with silver heels. She became a heroine by her services as a nurse in the smallpox epidemic in the mining camp called Buckskin Joe.

Silver Plume, town on U.S. 6 in Clear Creek County (est. 1870, inc. 1880, pop. 134). One story is that the name honors a national political figure, James G. Blaine (1830–93), known as the "Plumed Knight." Another is that the name was first applied to a mine in the district as the white streaks of silver appeared plume-like in the rocks.

Silverthorne, in Summit County (est. 1962, inc. 1967, pop. 1,768). Named for Marshall Silverthorn, who settled in Breckenridge in 1860. The spelling has fluctuated, with and without the final "e."

Silverton, town on U.S. 550 (est. 1874, inc. 1876, pop. 716); seat of San Juan County. The site was first known as Bakers Park; later names were Reeseville, Quito, and Greenville. In 1875, the name Silverton was chosen in an election, referring to the town's place in the San Juan silver mining region.

Simla [sim´ lə], town on U.S. 24 in Elbert County (est. 1888, inc. 1913, pop. 48). The railroad siding here was apparently named after the hill town of Simla in India, which was the summer capital of the British administration. The daughter of a Rock Island Railroad official is said to have suggested the name because it occurred in a book she was reading when her father noticed the siding from a train.

Skull Creek is the name of three streams in Colorado. One of them gives its name to a locale in Moffat County. The name may have been given on occasions when a skull was found in a creekbed.

Skunk. The striped species (*Mephitis mephitis*) is common in Colorado, and has given its name to seven streams called **Skunk Creek.**

Skyway, in Mesa County (post office est. 1927). This summer resort on Grand Mesa was named in honor of the Skyway Drive over the mountain. There is also a Skyway in El Paso County.

Slater, in Moffat County (est. 1876). Named for its founder, a trapper named William Slater.

Slick Rock, in San Miguel County (est. 1879), was first known as Snyder's Camp. The present name comes from a type of sandstone, called entrada sandstone by geologists; it is smooth and free of fractures.

Slumgullion [slum gul′ yən] **Pass,** in Hinsdale County (11,361 ft.), is named for the varicolored rocks of a vast, ancient slide (the Slumgullion Earth Flow), resembling the colors of a slumgullion stew. Derived from a word *gullion*, meaning a quagmire or cesspool, used in Scotland and Ireland.

Sneffels [snef′ əlz], a locale in Ouray County, is named for nearby **Mount Sneffels** (14,150 ft.). This in turn takes its name from a passage in Jules Verne's *Journey to the Center of the Earth,* mentioning the volcanic Mount Sneffels (or Snaefell) in Iceland as the entrance to the earth's core.

Sniktau [snik′ tou], **Mount,** in Clear Creek County (13,234 ft.), is said to be the "nom de plume" of E. H. N. Patterson, a pioneer journalist. He claimed it was an Indian word meaning "equal to any emergency." The similarity to the name of Sniktaw, California, may or may not be coincidental: the Californian name is supposed to represent the pseudonym of another pioneer journalist, W. F. Watkins, who obtained it by spelling his name backwards.

Snowmass, on Colorado 82 in Pitkin County (est. 1889), is named for **Snowmass Creek,** on which it borders. The stream is named in turn for **Snowmass Mountain** (14,092 ft.), in Gunnison and Pitkin counties, so called by Ferdinand V. Hayden for the mass of snow which gathered on the eastern side of the peak. The term "Twin Peaks" was once given to it along with Capitol Peak; later Snowmass Mountain was called Whitehouse Peak, before receiving its present name. **Snowmass Village,** a town and ski resort in Pitkin County (est. 1967, pop. 1,449), takes its name from the same source; it was formerly called Snowmass-at-Aspen.

Snyder, in Morgan County (est. 1882), was named for J. W. Snyder, a pioneer cattleman.

Somerset [sum′ ər set], on Colorado 133 in Gunnison County (est. 1902). After the coal fields of the North Fork Valley were opened, the Denver and Rio Grande Railroad established the town, naming it for a coal-mining community in Pennsylvania.

Sopris [sō′ pris], in Las Animas County. Named for General E. B. Sopris of the Colorado Militia. He also owned much of the coal land in the area. Separately named is **Mount Sopris,** in Pitkin County; this peak honors Richard Sopris, who headed a private party of fourteen men from Denver in July 1860, on an exploration trip to this area. **Sopris Creek** and **Lake** are in Eagle County.

Southern Ute Indian Reservation, in La Plata and Archuleta counties, is one of those established for the Utes, once the principal tribe of Colorado. They also give their name to the state of Utah.

South Fork, on U.S. 160 in Rio Grande County (est. 1880?), is an early stage station, named for its location where the South Fork of the Rio Grande joins the main stream.

Southglenn, a community in Arapahoe County (pop. 43,087). So named because it is south of Denver, as compared with Northglenn which is north of the city.

South Park is the high mountain valley from which the South Platte River rises. It is one of the major "parks" or open plains in Colorado, after which Park County was named. **South Park City** is in that county.

Spanish Peaks, between Huerfano and Las Animas counties, translates Spanish *Cumbres Españoles.* **West Spanish Peak** is 13,626 feet high; **East Spanish Peak,** 12,683 feet.

Spar City, in Mineral County (est. 1892), was originally named Fisher City after a discoverer of gold in the area. The name was later changed in reference to the Big Spar mine nearby. "Spar" is a Cornish name for quartz, which abounds in the area.

Spikebuck, on the Arkansas River and U.S. 50 in Fremont County, refers to a young male deer with unbranched antlers.

Spinney Mountain, in Park County (9,524 ft.). Named for B. F. Spinney, a land owner who arranged for a "Flower Train" excursion to be run to the site for the picking of wild flowers.

Spivak [spē′ vak], in Jefferson County, was named for Dr. Charles D. Spivak, a founder of the sanatorium of the Jewish Consumptives Relief Society.

Spring Creek is the name of thirty-three streams in Colorado. **Spring Creek Pass** is in Hinsdale County (10,898 ft.).

Springfield, town on U.S. 287 and 385 (est. 1887, inc. 1889, pop. 1,475); seat of Baca County. The townsite promoters purchased the tract from Andrew Harrison, a native of Springfield, Missouri. The new town was given the name of his home.

Squaw Pass, in Clear Creek County (9,790 ft.), was formerly known as Soda Hill Pass. The present name was adopted by the Colorado Geographic Board in 1916, presumably desiring a name with Indian associations. The term "squaw," meaning an Indian woman, is from Algonkian; at present its use is considered derogatory.

Star Mountain, in Lake County (12,941 ft.), was named by members of the Hayden exploring party around 1872, supposedly because they reached the summit just as the evening star appeared in the sky.

Starkville, on U.S. 85 and 87 in Las Animas County (est. 1879, inc. 1954, pop. 104). The first coal mine in the area was opened here about 1879 by H. G. Stark, and was known as the Starkville Mine. The settlement, originally called San Pedro, was then renamed in honor of Stark.

State Bridge, on Colorado 131 in Eagle County (est. 1889). The long-span bridge, constructed across the Colorado River here from 1889 to 1891, was the first state-financed bridge on the Western slope.

Steamboat Springs, city on U.S. 40 and the Yampa River (est. 1875, inc. 1907, pop. 6,695); seat of Routt County. The name is derived from the peculiar puffing sounds formerly emitted by one of the springs, resembling large river steamers in action. This spring was destroyed during the construction of the Moffat Railroad (now the Denver and Rio Grande Western) in 1908. **Steamboat Village** is nearby in Routt County.

Sterling, city on U.S. 6 (est. 1873, inc. 1884, pop. 10,362); seat of Logan County. A railroad surveyor, David Leavitt, liked the area so much that he started a ranch here. A post office was established on his ranch in 1872, and called Sterling for his hometown in Illinois.

Stewart Peak, in Saguache County (13,983 ft.). Named for William M. Stewart (1827–1909), a Nevada senator who advocated free silver.

Stoneham [stō´ nəm], in Weld County (est. 1888). Derived from Stone, the family name of an early settler.

Stoner, on Colorado 145 in Montezuma County (est. 1890?), was probably named for the creek upon which it is located. The stream has been known as **Stoner Creek** by residents in the area since 1888.

Stones Peak, in Larimer County (12,922 ft.), was named for the geologist G. M. Stone who visited it in 1886.

Stoneton, in Baca County (est. 1887), was named for a nearby stream which contained many rocks.

Stonewall, on Colorado 12 in Las Animas County (est. 1867). The first resident was Juan Gutiérrez, who built a cabin here in 1867 and began grazing cattle. The valley, for a time, was known in Spanish as *El Valle de Gutiérrez.* James Stoner homesteaded somewhat to the west; and because of a rock formation on his place, the region was known as Stoner's Wall. When the settlement needed a post office in 1878, the name became Stonewall.

Strasburg, on U.S. 36, 40, and 287 in Arapahoe County (est. 1890). Named for John Strasburg, who built a section of the track for the Union Pacific Railroad.

Stratton, town on U.S. 24 in Kit Carson County (est. 1888, inc. 1915, pop. 649). First known as Claremont. Named for Winfield Scott Stratton, a Colorado Springs carpenter who became a mining magnate after rich strikes in Cripple Creek. The town was supposedly named for him in the hope that he would donate money. While he did spend some time in the community, there is no record he gave funds. There is also a Stratton in Teller County.

Sugar City, town on state route 96 in Crowley County (est. 1891, inc. 1900, pop. 252). Founded by employees of the National Sugar Company, it takes its name from the large sugar factory established in the rich sugar beet region.

Sugar Loaf, also written Sugarloaf, is the name of seven prominences in Colorado, so called because of similarity in shape to the blocks in which sugar was formerly sold. One has given its name to a settlement in

Boulder County. There are also eleven peaks in the state called **Sugarloaf Mountain,** the highest of which is in Mineral County (12,593 ft.). In addition, there are six prominences called **Sugarloaf Peak,** the highest being in San Juan County (12,545 ft.).

Summit County (est. 1861, area 604 sq. mi., pop. 12,881). The county seat is Breckenridge. Named for the high altitude of the area. Summit County was one of the original seventeen territorial counties; portions were used to create other counties. **Summit Springs Battlefield** is on the border between Logan and Washington counties; it was the scene of the last major battle between the Cheyenne Indians and the U.S. Cavalry. **Summitville** is in Rio Grande County (est. 1872). Once called Summit, it was probably named because of its altitude (11,300 ft.). Located near the crest of the Continental Divide.

Sunbeam, on Colorado 318 in Moffat County (est. 1912). When the post office was established, N. C. Bonivee, a farmer, suggested the name: he claimed that the sun shone more brightly on this particular spot than anywhere else in the area.

Sundance Mountain, in Rocky Mountain National Park, Larimer County (12,470 ft.), is apparently named after a major ceremony of the Plains Indian tribes.

Sunetha [sə nē′ thə] **Flats,** in Archuleta County, is said to have been coined by combing elements from the names of three early settlers: Sullenberger, Newton, and Hatcher.

Sunlight Peak, in La Plata County (14,059 ft.), was named by the U.S. Geological Survey in 1902; possibly the peak was flooded with sunshine when it was surveyed.

Sunshine Peak, in Hinsdale County (14,001 ft.), was named by the U.S. Geological Survey about 1904. Earlier it was known as Niagra Peak or Sherman Peak.

Superior, in Boulder County (est. 1897, inc. 1904, pop. 255), was probably named for Superior, Wisconsin. However, another story is that a "Mr. Hake," who owned a coal mine, named it for a Nebraska town he liked.

Swallows, on the Arkansas River in Pueblo County, is named for the thousands of cliff swallows, *Petrochelidon pyrrhonota,* which nest in the limestone bluffs along the river.

Sweetwater, in Eagle County. The term designates water suitable for drinking, as opposed to salty or alkaline water.

Swink, town on U.S. 50 in Otero County (est. 1900, inc. 1900, pop. 584). Named for State Senator George W. Swink (1893–97), a farmer as well as legislator. The settlement was previously called Fairmont.

Switzerland Park, in Boulder County, is named for the **Switzerland Trail,** a former railroad line that linked Boulder with the mining camps of Sugarloaf, Eldora, Ward, and Blue Bird.

Tabeguache [tāb´ wäch] **Peak,** in Chaffee County (14,155 ft.). A shortened form of the name of a band of Ute Indians. The full Ute name was *mogwatavüngwantsingwü* "cedar-bark sun-slope people." The mountain was known but unnamed for many years.

Tabernash [tab´ ər nash], on U.S. 40 in Grand County (est. 1905). Located on the old Junction Ranch, homestead of Edward J. Vulgamott, an 1882 pioneer. In 1879 a Ute Indian called Tabernash was killed here by a white man named "Big Frank"; the killing was a forerunner of the Meeker and Thornburg massacres. E. A. Meredith, chief engineer of the Denver and Salt Lake Railroad, named the settlement for the murdered Indian. The Ute name was perhaps *tapö´n´ach* "having a cramp."

Table Mesa, an area in the city of Boulder. Since *mesa* is Spanish for "table," local wags call the area "Tisch Tisch" (German *Tisch* "table"). **Table Mountain** is the name of eight peaks in Colorado; the highest is in Mineral County (12,860 ft.).

Tacoma [tə kō´ mə], in La Plata County, was perhaps named after the city in Washington State; the term is derived from an Indian name for Mount Rainier.

Tahosa [tə hō´ sə] **Valley,** in Larimer and Boulder counties, east of Longs Peak. Supposedly an Indian word meaning "dwellers on the mountaintops," and once seriously considered by Congress for the territory admitted to the Union under the name Colorado. Possibly a Kiowa name, since a Kiowa had signed a treaty in 1837 as "Tahosa, the Top of the Mountains."

Talamantes [tal ə man′ tēz] **Creek,** in Moffat County, is said to be the name of an Indian chief. In origin, however, it is a Spanish family name.

Talahassee [tal ə has′ ē] **Creek,** a tributary of the Arkansas River, in Fremont County. Probably named for the city in Florida, where it is taken in turn from a Muskogee Indian name meaning "old town."

Tanima [tə nī′ mə] **Peak,** in Rocky Mountain National Park, Boulder County (12,420 ft.). Named for a band of the Comanche Indian tribe, called *tanümütühka* "liver-eaters."

Tarryall [târ′ ē ôl], in Park County. It is said that a group discovered gold here; and believing there was enough for everyone, gave the camp the name "Tarry-all."

Taylor Park, in Gunnison County, was named for Jim Taylor, a miner who arrived in 1860. **Taylor Peak,** in Rocky Mountain National Park, between Grand and Larimer counties (13,153 ft.), was named for Albert Reynolds Taylor, an educator from Kansas who visited the area in 1895.

Teds Place, in Larimer County (est. 1922). Founded by Edward Irving Herring, better known as Ted, when he returned from World War I.

Teller County (est. 1899, area 553 sq. mi., pop. 12,468). The county seat is Cripple Creek. In honor of U.S. Senator Henry M. Teller (1830–1914), called the "Silver Senator" because of his role in advocating free silver. The county was formed from portions of El Paso and Fremont counties.

Telluride [tel′ yōō rīd], town on Colorado 145 (est. 1878, inc. 1887, pop. 1,309); seat of San Miguel County. Founded as Columbia, its growth was slow until the Denver and Rio Grande Southern Railroad was completed in 1890. The name was changed to Telluride, referring to the tellurium ore found in the vicinity. Tellurium is a rare element related to sulphur, usually combined with metals such as gold and silver. **Telluride Peak** is in Ouray County (13,509 ft.).

Templeton, in El Paso County, may have been named for A. J. Templeton, an early resident.

Tenderfoot Mountain is the name of nine peaks in Colorado; the highest is in Summit County (11,441 ft.). The term designates an inexperienced person.

Tennessee Pass, on the Continental Divide, between Eagle and Lake counties (10,424 ft.). Named in the 1860s, supposedly by goldminers from the southern state. The name is said to be originally that of a Cherokee chief.

Teocalli [tē ō kä′ lē] **Mountain,** in Gunnison County (13,208 ft.). The Aztec word for "temple," analyzable as *teo-calli* "god-house."

Tercio [tûr′ sē ō], in Las Animas County. Spanish for "third," because it was the third of five mining operations opened in that area by the Colorado Fuel and Iron Company in 1904.

Terra Tomah [târ ə tō′ mə] **Mountain,** in Rocky Mountain National Park, Larimer County (12,718 ft.). In the summer of 1914, George Barnard, hiking with the Colorado Mountain Club, sighted a lake near this mountain, and sang a supposed Indian song with the words "He ne Terratoma, ne terratoma." James Grafton Rogers, President of the Club, proposed Terra Tomah to the federal government as the name of the lake, but by mistake it was assigned to the mountain. (The body of water was subsequently named Doughnut Lake.) The song supposedly came from the Cahuilla Indians of Southern California, and Barnard had learned it when he was a student there at Pomona College. The anthropologist David Prescott Barrows, who worked with the Cahuilla and taught the song to Pomona College students, said he was not able to obtain an interpretation of the words from his Indian consultants.

Texas Creek is the name of seven streams in Colorado; one of them gave its name to **Texas Creek,** a locale in Fremont County (est. 1879?). The stream was named by Joseph Lamb, who camped there while driving cattle north from Texas. The name of the state of Texas is from an Indian word *teyas* "friends," first recorded in 1541, when it was taken to be a tribal name.

Thatcher, in Las Animas County (est. 1880?). Originally a stage-station known as Hole-in-the-Rock, because of a natural spring where the stage horses were watered. The name was changed after several years to honor M. D. Thatcher, pioneer banker and businessman of southern Colorado.

Thatchtop, a peak in Rocky Mountain National Park, Larimer County (12,668 ft.). Named for the matted groundcover on the roof-shaped mountain.

Thornton, city in Adams County (est. 1952, inc. 1956, pop. 55,031). Named to honor Governor Dan Thornton, who was in office at the time the community was established.

Thorodin [thōr′ ō din] **Mountain,** in Gilpin County (10,509 ft.). Perhaps named for the ancient Norse gods Thor and Odin.

Tiffany, in La Plata County, was named for Ed Tiffany, a civil engineer.

Tiger, in Summit County, was named after the Royal Tiger Mines Company.

Tigiwon [tig′ i won], in Eagle County, has been the base camp of the Mount of the Holy Cross pilgrimage since 1927. Camp Fire girls from Gypsum selected the name, representing Ute *tügü′vün* "friend."

Tijeras [tē hâr′ əs], on Colorado 12 in Las Animas County, is Spanish for "scissors"; also a family name.

Timnath [tim′ nath], town in Larimer County (est. 1882, inc. 1920, pop. 190). Named by the Reverend Charles A. Taylor, the first Presbyterian minister, with the biblical name from the Book of Judges 14.5: "And Samson went down to Timnath," a Philistine city where he saw a woman he later married.

Timpas [tim′ pəs], on U.S. 350 in Otero County (est. 1868). For **Timpas Creek,** a tributary of the Arkansas River. Spanish *timpa*, English "tymp" means "bar of stone or iron in a blast furnace." Curiously, Southern Paiute *tümp* means "stone, iron" (cf. Ute *tüpúich* "stone").

Tincup, in Gunnison County (est. 1879). Named in 1861 when a prospector returned from here with gold-bearing earth in a tin cup.

Tiny Town, in Jefferson County (est. 1915). An elaborate miniature city built by George E. Turner on the banks of Turkey Creek. A resort village grew up around the small-scale community, and retained the Tiny Town name.

Tioga [tī ō′ gə], in Huerfano County. Named for a place in Pennsylvania, originally an Iroquois word meaning "at the forks."

Tobe [tōb], on U.S. 160 in Las Animas County (post office est. 1910). Named for Tobe Benavides, a local resident. When "Benavides" was submitted as the name for the settlement, the post office chose "Tobe" instead.

Toll, Mount, on the Continental Divide between Grand and Boulder counties (12,979 ft.). Named for Roger Toll, mountaineer and superintendent of Rocky Mountain National Park from 1921 to 1929.

Tolland [tō´ lənd], in Gilpin County. Named by Mrs. Charles H. Toll after Tolland, England, the home of her ancestors.

Toltec [tol´ tek], in Huerfano County. From the Aztec word *tolteca,* designating an ancient people of Mexico. The literal meaning is "people of the *tules* or reeds."

Tomichi [tō mē´ chē] **Dome,** in Gunnison County (11,465 ft.). Tomichi was reported by the 1776 Dominguez-Escalante Expedition as the Indian name for the Gunnison River. Probably from Ute *tumúchich* "dome-shaped rock."

Tonahutu [tun ə hoo´ too] **Creek,** in Rocky Mountain National Park, Grand County. From Arapaho *toonoxtééni'* "meadow."

Toonerville, on Colorado 101 in Bent County (est. 1928). Named for the "Toonerville Trolley" in a nationally syndicated comic strip created by Fontaine Fox .

Toponas [tə pō´ nəs], on Colorado 131 in Routt County (est. 1888), is named from the nearby **Toponas Rock.** A Ute word of uncertain meaning.

Torres [tō´ rəs] is the name of places in both Rio Grande and Las Animas counties. The name is a common Spanish surname, originally meaning "towers."

Torreys Peak, in Clear Creek and Summit counties (14,267 ft.). Named by C. C. Parry for the botanist John Torrey. Torrey and Asa Gray collaborated in 1831 on the first part of the *Flora of North America,* and have been called America's first botanists.

Towaoc [tō´ ā ok], on the Ute Mountain Indian Reservation in Montezuma County (est. 1920, pop. 700); also pronounced [toi´ ok]. From Ute *tüwáyak* "all right," also used to mean "thank you"; derived from *tüü'ay* "it's good." Suposedly the word expressed the Indians' approval when the Ute Mountain sub-agency was moved here from Navajo Springs.

Towner, in Kiowa County (est. 1887?), was founded by the Missouri Pacific Railroad and named for a railroad official. Earlier, the community was known as Memphis.

Trachyte [trā´ kīt] **Knob,** a peak in Teller County (10,862 ft.). The term refers to a type of volcanic rock.

Trail Ridge, in Larimer County, gives its name to the pass called **Trail Ridge High Point** (12,183 ft.), so called for its route in traversing part of an old Indian ridge trail. **Trail Ridge Road** is the highest continuous highway in the United States.

Trementina Creek, in Las Animas County, contains the Spanish word for "turpentine."

Trimble, on U.S. 550 in La Plata County. Named for Frank Trimble, who discovered hot springs on his ranch here.

Trinchera [trin châr´ ə], in Las Animas County (est. 1873?). The name is a Spanish word meaning "trench" or "entrenchment"; it was given to the village because of a gap or pass through a nearby mesa. Earlier it was known as San Jose and Grinell. **Trinchera Peak** is in Costilla County (13,517 ft.).

Trinidad [trin´ i dad], city on U.S. 85, 87, and 160 (est. 1859, inc. 1879, pop. 8,580); seat of Las Animas County. Its first name, when the first cabin was built by Gabriel and Juan N. Gutiérrez, was Río de Las Animas. It then became a favorite rendezvous for early trappers, traders, and travelers, and was called *Santísima Trinidad* "most holy trinity."

Troublesome, on U.S. 40 in Grand County. Named for nearby **Troublesome Creek,** so called by soldiers who were forced to make long detours to cross the stream.

Troy, in Las Animas County. Named for the ancient site of the Trojan War, as described in Homer's *Iliad.*

Trujillo [trōō hē´ ō], on the San Juan River in Archuleta County, is derived from a common Spanish surname. There is also a **Trujillo Creek** in Las Animas County.

Tungsten, on Colorado 119 in Boulder County, is named for tungsten mines which were active here during World War I.

Turquoise Lake, in Lake County, is named for its color, not for the semiprecious stone.

Turret is in Chaffee County. A rocky promontory here is said to resemble a turret on a battleship.

Tweto, Mount, in Lake County (13,672 ft.), is named for the geologist Ogden Tweto.

Twin Lakes is the name of eleven paired bodies of water in Colorado. One of them gives its name to **Twin Lakes,** a locale on Colorado 82 in Lake County (est. 1880?).

Twin Peaks is the name of seven geological features in Colorado; the highest is in Alamosa County (13,580 ft.).

Two Buttes [byōōts], town on Colorado 116 in Baca County (est. 1909, inc. 1911, pop. 63). Named for the striking buttes near the Baca and Prowers county line, about thirteen miles north of the town.

Tyndall Creek, in Rocky Mountain National Park, Larimer County. Named for John Tyndall (1820–93), an English physicist and student of glacial phenomena.

Tyrone [tə rōn´], on Colorado 350 in Las Animas County (post office est. 1916). Founded as Yetta, and changed in 1929. Tyrone is a county in Ireland, but its name has been used for other places in the U.S. (e.g., in Pennsylvania).

Uintah Range, [yōō in´ tə] in Moffat County, is mostly in the state of Utah. The Ute name, *yüvintü,* means "pine canyon-mouth."

Una [yōō´ nə], in Garfield County. Spanish for "one" (fem.), given to section house number one on the Denver and Rio Grande Railroad.

Unaweep [yōō´ nə wēp] **Canyon,** in Mesa County, following West Creek (which flows to the Dolores River) and East Creek (which flows to the Gunnison River), with **Unaweep Divide** between them. Perhaps from Ute *kuná-wiiyap* "fire canyon," because of the red color.

Uncompahgre [un kəm pä′ grē] **Peak,** in Hinsdale County (14,309 ft.). For the **Uncompahgre River** (in Delta, Montrose, and San Juan counties), named by the Ute Indians. The name was recorded by the Dominguez-Escalante expedition in 1776 as Ancapagari, translated *Laguna Colorada* "red lake." A present-day Ute pronunciation is *aká-paagarür* ; cf. *aká-gar* "red," *páagarür* "lake."

Uneva Peak, in Summit County (12,522 ft.). Perhaps from Ute *yunáv* "mountainous country."

Uravan [o͞or′ ə van], on the San Miguel River and Colorado 141 in Montrose County (est. 1912?). Named in 1936 when the United States Vanadium Corporation began work here. The name Uravan is derived from the first syllables of uranium and vanadium, elements occurring in carnotite ore. Carnotite was first mined here in 1881 for the small amounts of gold found in it. In 1898 the Smithsonian Institution found that the ore contained uranium, and several tons were shipped to France. Madame Curie used this ore in her experiments that resulted in the extraction of radium.

Urraca [yo͞o rak′ ə] **Creek,** in Alamosa County; from the Spanish for "magpie." A pronunciation closer to Spanish would be [o͞o rä′ kä].

Ute [yo͞ot], in Montrose County. Named for the principal Indian tribe of Colorado, which formerly occupied the state from the Front Range westward. Members now live at the **Ute Mountain Indian Reservation,** in Montezuma County; at the **Southern Ute Indian Reservation,** in La Plata and San Juan counties; and in the state of Utah. The term "Ute" is a shortening of a tribal designation "Utah" (from which comes the name of the state). The term entered English from New Mexico Spanish *yuta,* which reflects the name given to the tribe in several Indian languages of the Southwest. Many geographical features in Colorado are named for this tribe; thus **Ute Creek** is the name of fourteen streams. Three mountains are called **Ute Peak,** the highest of which is in Mineral County (12,303 ft.). There is a **Ute Mountain** in Boulder County (9,782 ft.). The name **Ute Pass** exists in five locations; the highest of these is in Saguache County (11,100 ft.).

Utleyville, on U.S. 160 in Baca County (est. 1918), was named after A. H. Utley, the first postmaster.

Vachita [və chē′ tə] **Creek,** in Las Animas County. A corruption of Bachicha, a Spanish family name.

Vail, town on U.S. 6 in Eagle County (est. 1959, inc. 1966, pop. 3,659). Named for nearby **Vail Pass** (10,666 ft.), which was in turn named for Charles D. Vail, Colorado state highway engineer who planned it in the 1930s.

Valdez [val dez′], in Las Animas County. Named for Gabriel Valdez, who homesteaded there about 1900.

Vallecito [vī yə sē′ tō], in La Plata County; also pronounced [vī sē′ tō]. Spanish for "little valley," the diminutive of *valle* "valley."

Vallejos [vä yā′ hōs] **Creek,** in Costilla County. Perhaps the plural of the Spanish family name *Vallejo.*

Valle Seco [vä′ yā sā′ kō], a valley in Archuleta County. Spanish for "dry valley."

Vallorso [val ōr′ sō], in Las Animas County. Perhaps from Italian *Vall'Orso* "Bear Valley."

Valmont, in Boulder County. Supposedly named after the adjacent valleys and mountains. The town was laid out in 1865, and was once larger than Boulder.

Vanadium [və nā′ di yəm], in San Miguel County, is a rare element used in making steel.

Vancorum, in Montrose County (est. 1930), was founded by and for the Vanadium Corporation of America. The name is an acronym using the first letters of the corporate name. Sometime during the years, however, the "am" became "um" on the map.

Vandiver [van′ də vûr] **Arroyo,** in Otero County, was named for a family which homesteaded here in 1882.

Vasquez [vas′ kəz] **Peak,** in Clear Creek County (12,947 ft.). Perhaps for Louis Vasquez, who built a fort on Clear Creek in 1832; or for his brother Antoine F. Vasquez, an interpreter for Lieutenant Zebulon Pike.

Vega Canyon, in Las Animas County. The Spanish word means "a fertile plain"; in the Spanish of New Mexico and Colorado, it specifically refers to pastureland.

Vermejo Peak, in Costilla County (13,723 ft.). For Spanish *bermejo* "a shade of red."

Vernon, in Yuma County (est. 1892), was formerly called Condon's Corners, after Barney Condon, founder of the *Wray Rattler* newspaper (1886–1948). When the present site was laid out by a townsite committee, each member proposed a name. T. A. Wilson's suggestion was agreed upon, perhaps recalling George Washington's home at Mount Vernon in Virginia.

Victor, city in Teller County (est. 1893, inc. 1894, pop. 258). Early known as the City of Mines, and named for the Victor Mine.

Viejo San Acacio, in Costilla County. Spanish for "Old" San Acacio.

Vigil [və hēl´], on Colorado 12 in Las Animas County. Named for Cornelio Vigil, one of the partners to whom the Vigil and Saint Vrain Land Grant was made. **Mount Vigil** is in El Paso County (10,073 ft.).

Vilas [vī´ ləs], town on U.S. 160 in Baca County (est. 1888, inc. 1888, pop. 105). Named for William F. Vilas of Wisconsin, secretary of the interior (1888–89) under President Grover Cleveland. Prior to this he was postmaster general, and this could be the reason the community was named for him.

Villa Grove, in Saguache County (est. 1870). Earlier known as Garibaldi. The present name was given in 1872, based on Italian *villa* "country house," with reference to a beautiful grove that surrounded the original townsite.

Villegreen [vil ə grēn´], in Las Animas County (est. 1917). A name coined by the postal authorities when they rejected a list of possible names submitted by the community's residents. The term is a combination of French *ville* "town" with the name of J. L. Greene, the first postmaster.

Vineland, on U.S. 50 in Pueblo County (est. 1876). Named for early vineyards in the area.

Virginia Dale, on U.S. 287 in Larimer County (est. 1862). Named by founder Joseph A. ("Jack") Slade for his wife, Virginia Dale.

Vona [vō´ nə], on U.S. 24 in Kit Carson County (est. 1888, inc. 1919, pop. 104). The town was promoted by Pearl S. King, an attorney from Burlington, Colorado, and was named for his niece Vona.

Vroman [vrō´ mən], on U.S. 50 in Otero County. Called Witzer, for a German farmer, until World War I, when, because of anti-German feeling, it was renamed for John C. Vroman, an early landowner.

Vulcan, in Gunnison County. Named in 1895 for the nearby Vulcan Mine, recalling the ancient Roman god of metal-working.

Wagon Wheel Gap, on Colorado 149 in Mineral County (est. 1872?). The name is derived from a large wagon wheel found here, supposed to have been left by the Baker prospecting party of 1861, on their way out of the mountains.

Wahatoya [wä hä toi´ yə] **Creek,** in Huerfano County. An alternative spelling of the name Guajatoyah, also found in Las Animas County. Ute for "twin mountains."

Walden, town on Colorado 125 (est. 1889, inc. 1890, pop. 890); seat of Jackson County. Once known as Sagebrush. The present name honors Mark A. Walden, one-time postmaster at Sage Hen Springs, about four miles southwest.

Wallstreet, in Boulder County. A former gold mine, invested in by New Yorkers who gave it its name.

Walsenburg [wôl´ sən bûrg], city on U.S. 85, 87, and 160 (est. 1873, inc. 1873, pop. 3,300); seat of Huerfano County. Founded as La Plaza de los Leones, named for Don Miguel Antonio León, an early settler. In 1870, Fred Walsen opened a general store and became a community leader. When the village was incorporated, the name was changed in his honor. In 1887, postal authorities changed the name to Tourist City; but indignant citizens demanded the return of the old name.

Walsh, town on U.S. 160 in Baca County (est. 1914, inc. 1928, pop. 692). Named for a retired general baggage agent of the Atchison, Topeka, and Santa Fe Railway.

Ward, town on Colorado 72 in Boulder County (est. 1865, inc. 1896, pop. 159). Named for Calvin W. Ward, who in 1860 discovered the gold-bearing seam known as the Ward Lode. The now-abandoned Denver, Boulder and

Western Railroad (the "Switzerland Trail of America") made daily runs between Ward and Boulder.

Wasatch [wä´ sach] **Mountain,** in San Miguel County (13,555 ft.). The name of a Ute chief who lived around 1800; his name is also given to the Wasatch Mountain Range in Utah.

Washington County (est. 1887, area 2,526 sq. mi., pop. 4,812). The county seat is Akron. Named for President George Washington (1732–99); previously part of Weld County.

Watanga [wə täng´ gə] **Mountain,** in Grand County (12,375 ft.). Said to be an abbreviation of the name of an Arapaho leader, *wo'atáánkoo'óh,* literally "Black Coyote."

Watha Gulch, in Larimer County. Perhaps from Arapaho *wôoxe* "knife."

Watkins, in Adams County (est. 1872). Established by the Kansas Pacific Railroad (now part of the Union Pacific system), it was first called Box Elder. Later it was renamed for L. A. Watkins, a local rancher and merchant.

Waunita [wô nē´ tə] **Hot Springs,** in Gunnison County (est. 1884). When the medicinal springs were purchased in 1884 by Dr. Charles G. Davis of Chicago, he changed the name from Tomichi Hot Springs to Waunita Hot Springs, supposedly after an Indian woman. The name may be a respelling of Juanita, a Spanish woman's name, familiar from a popular song of the nineteenth century. **Wauneta,** on U.S. 385 in Yuma County, may be a form of the same name.

Waverly, on state route 370 in Alamosa County, is probably named after the series of popular novels by Sir Walter Scott. There is also a Waverly in Larimer County.

Welby, in Adams County (pop. 10,218). Named for General Welby, president of the Denver, Laramie and Northwest Railroad.

Weld County (est. 1861, area 4,002 sq. mi., pop. 131,821). The county seat is Greeley. Named for Lewis Ledyard Weld, first secretary of Colorado Territory. It was one of the seventeen original territorial counties.

Weldona [wel dō´ nə], on Colorado 144 in Morgan County (est. 1866). Originally called Weldon, either for a resident or for an army general named Weldon. Later it was known as Deuel; but it was later changed to Weldona, the letter "a" being added to reduce confusion with the town of Walden.

Wellington, on Colorado 1 in Larimer County (est. 1902, inc. 1905, pop. 1,340). Named for a traffic manager of the Colorado and Southern Railway.

Weminuche [wem i nōō′ chē] **Creek,** in Hinsdale County; also **Weminuche Wilderness,** in Hinsdale, San Juan, and La Plata counties (on map). Named after a band of the Ute Indian tribe. The native name, *wimünuchi,* is of unknown meaning.

Westcliffe, town on Colorado 69 (est. 1885, inc. 1897, pop. 312); seat of Custer County. Known first as Clifton, the town was renamed by Dr. W. A. Bell for his birthplace, Westcliff-on-the-Sea, England.

West Creek is the name of six streams in Colorado. One of them gave its name to **Westcreek,** a locale in Douglas County (est. 1895?). The town was named for the district, in turn named for West Creek, a small tributary of Horse Creek, flowing through the town. The official post office name, however, was Pemberton, which honored the first owner of the site. It was a several years later before the post office name was changed.

West Elk Mountains and **Wilderness Area,** west and south of Crested Butte in Gunnison County. **West Elk Peak** (13,035 ft.) is also here. **West Elk Creek** and the nearby East Elk Creek are in this area; there is no "Elk Creek" in the region.

Westminster [west min′ stər], city on U.S. 287 in Adams and Jefferson counties (est. 1891, inc. 1909, pop. 74,625). The land was once owned by a man named Harris. When the community grew large enough to accommodate a store and post office, it was called Harris Park. In 1891, Stanford White of New York organized a Presbyterian college; he named it Westminster, and the settlement was incorporated with this name.

Weston, on Colorado 12 in Las Animas County (est. 1860?). Settled in the 1880s by a family headed by Juan Sisneros, a rancher. Though scarcely more than a plaza, it was given the name Los Sisneros. There was no post office until about 1892, when Bert Weston, a blacksmith, was granted the office of postmaster. The town then became known as Weston. **Weston Pass** is between Lake and Park counties (11,900 ft.).

Wetmore, on Colorado 96 in Custer County (est. 1880?). The site of a stage coach station in pioneer days. William Hayes homesteaded 160 acres in 1880. He sold the site to Frances Wetmore, whose husband, William, surveyed and named the townsite.

Wet Mountains, a range in Custer County. The name translates Spanish *Sierra Mojada,* so called because of the well-watered terrain.

Wetterhorn Peak, in Hinsdale and Ouray counties (14,015 ft.). Thought to have been named by the Wheeler Survey of 1874 for the well-known peak in the Swiss Alps, which it somewhat resembles.

Wheat Ridge, city in Jefferson County (est. 1862?, inc. 1969, pop. 29,419). Named by State Senator Henry Lee because this was a thriving wheat growing area.

Wheeler Junction, on U.S. 6, at the junction of West Ten Mile and Ten Mile Creeks, in Summit County (est. 1880). Founded by homesteader John S. Wheeler, after whom the post office was named.

White River, a stream in Rio Blanco County; the English name is a translation of the Spanish name still used for the county.

Whitewater, on U.S. 50 in Mesa County (est. 1884?). The name comes from Whitewater Creek, so called because of the high alkali content.

Widefield, on U.S. 85 and 87 in El Paso County. The twin community of Security-Widefield has a population of 23,822.

Wiggins, town on U.S. 6 and 34 in Morgan County (est. 1894?, inc. 1974, pop. 499). Named for Major Oliver P. Wiggins, better known as "old Scout" Wiggins. A Canadian and once an employee of the Hudson Bay Company, he came to Colorado about 1834. The town was called Vallery and then Corona, before it became Wiggins about 1894.

Wild Horse, on U.S. 40 and 287 in Cheyenne County (est. 1860?). From nearby **Wild Horse Creek,** once a watering place for immense bands of wild horses. There is another Wild Horse in Pueblo County.

Wiley, town on Colorado 196 in Prowers County (est. 1899, inc. 1909, pop. 406). The settlement was named for W. M. Wiley, one of the town's promoters.

Willard, in Logan County (est. 1888), was named for Daniel Willard, president of the Burlington Railroad.

Williamsburg, town in Fremont County (est. 1880, inc. 1888, pop. 253). Named for John Williams, who opened the Williamsburg Mine for the Colorado Fuel & Iron Company.

Willow Creek is the name of thirty-five streams in Colorado. **Willow Creek Pass** is on the Continental Divide, between Grand and Jackson counties (9,621 ft.).

Wilson, Mount, in Dolores County (14,246 ft.). Named for A. D. Wilson, chief topographer for the Hayden Survey in 1874, who climbed the peak in that year. Nearby **Wilson Peak,** in San Miguel County (14,017 ft.) is named for the same mountaineer.

Windom Peak, in La Plata County (14,082 ft.). Named for William Windom (1827–91), who was a U.S. representative and senator (though not from Colorado) and secretary of the treasury under President Garfield.

Windsor, town on Colorado 257 and 392 in Weld County (est. 1882, inc. 1890, pop. 5,062). B. H. Eaton, later a state governor (1884–86) established a farm on the present site in 1863. In 1880 the post office was called New Liberty, and in January, 1884, postal authorities called it New Windsor, but the town was incorporated as Windsor. The name honors the Reverend A. S. Windsor of Fort Collins, a Methodist circuit minister.

Winter Park, town in Grand County (est. 1923, pop. 528), came into existence as a construction camp for the Moffat Tunnel, the west portal of which is here. It was first called West Portal; but with the consent of postal authorities, the name was changed to Winter Park, to publicize establishment of the winter sports area.

Wolcott, in Eagle County (est. 1889), was first known as Bussells. The present name honors Edward O. Wolcott, U.S. senator from Colorado from 1879 to 1883.

Wolf Creek is the name of twelve streams in Colorado. **Wolf Creek Pass** is on the Continental Divide, in Mineral County (10,850 ft.). Named for the stream on the west side, probably for timber wolves in the area. The wolf is now probably extinct in Colorado.

Wondervu [wun´ dər vyōō], in Boulder County, was named for its spectacular view of the Continental Divide.

Woodland Park, city on Colorado 67 in Teller County (est. 1890, inc. 1891, pop. 4,610). Previously known as Summit Park and Manitou Park.

Woodrow, on Colorado 71 in Washington County (est. 1913). Settled by J. A. McGilvray in 1913, the year that Woodrow Wilson became president of the United States.

Woody Creek, a locale in Pitkin County (est. 1890), takes its name from a nearby stream, probably so called because of the forested nature of the area.

Wootton, in Las Animas County, was named for Richens L. ("Uncle Dick") Wootton, a frontier scout.

Wray, city on U.S. 34 (est. 1886, inc. 1906, pop. 1,998); seat of Yuma County. Named for John Wray, foreman for I. P. Olive, one of the earliest ranchers in the county.

Wuh [wōō], **Mount,** in Rocky Mountain National Park, Larimer County (10,761 ft.). From Arapaho *wox* "bear."

Xenia [zē´ nyə], in Washington County. Perhaps from Xenia, Ohio. In Russian, a common given name for a woman.

Yale, in Kit Carson County (post office est. 1889), was named for a settler, William Henry Yale. Separately named is **Mount Yale,** in Chaffee County (14,196 ft.), the third peak in the Collegiate Group, named by Professor Josiah D. Whitney. He was a graduate of Yale University, head of the Harvard Mining School, and head of an 1869 survey sponsored by Harvard.

Yampa [yam´ pə], town on Colorado 131 in Routt County (est. 1882, inc. 1907, pop. 317). Named for the Yamparikach division of the Ute Indians, who lived in eastern Utah. They in turn were named after a plant with an edible root (formerly called *Carum gairdneri,* now *Perideridia gairdneri*), known locally in English as "yampa," "yamp," "yant," or "nant," reflecting Ute *nanta, yanta, yampa,* or Shoshone *wampa.* The **Yampa River** is in Moffatt and Routt counties.

Yarmony [yär´ mə nē], in Eagle County. Named for a Ute chief called Yarmony or Yarmonite, from Ute *yáamani* "quiet man."

Yellow Jacket, on U.S. 666 in Montezuma County (est. 1914). When a post office was organized in 1914, the name Yellow Jacket was given for a nearby canyon, the walls of which were plastered with yellow jacket nests.

Yoder [yō´ dər], on Colorado 94 in El Paso County (est. 1904). Named for Ira M. Yoder, a German homesteader, who was active in obtaining a post office for his community.

Ypsilon [ip´ si lən] **Mountain,** in Rocky Mountain National Park, Larimer County (13,514 ft.). The word is Greek for the letter Y, because of a Y-shaped snowfield on the face of the mountain. However, "ypsilon" is the German name for this letter; the usual name in English is "upsilon."

Yucca House National Monument, in Montezuma County. "Yucca" here refers to the flowering plant otherwise known as Spanish bayonet, *Yucca glauca.* The English word is borrowed from Spanish, which probably took in turn from an American Indian language of the West Indies.

Yuma [yōō´ mə], city on U.S. 34 in Yuma County (est. 1886; 1887, pop. 2,719). The townsite was established by Fred Weld and Ida P. Alrich. The name is said to come from "Yuma Switch," a nearby siding on the Burlington Railroad. When the track was laid here in the 1880s, a number of Indians from the Yuma tribe of Arizona were employed as laborers, and one of them died at this particular switch. The name was also given to **Yuma County** (est. 1889, area 2,379 sq. mi., pop. 8,954), although the county seat is not Yuma, but Wray. Formed from part of Washington County.

Zion, **Mount,** is the name of two peaks in Colorado; the higher is in Lake County (12,126 ft.). Mount Zion was originally the hill in Jerusalem on which the Jews built their temple.

Zirkel [zûr′ kəl], **Mount,** on Continental Divide between Routt and Jackson counties (12,180 ft.). Named by Clarence King for Ferdinand Zirkel, a German petrologist who in 1874 contributed his expertise to King's Fortieth Parallel Survey.

ACKNOWLEDGMENTS

Grateful recognition is made of the advice and information provided by the following local historians, librarians, and language scholars. Errors found in this book are the responsibility of the author alone.

Arlène Ahlbrandt, Fort Collins (Larimer County).

James Armagost, Linguistics Program, Kansas State University, Manhattan, KS (Comanche language).

Laura Bennhoff, Director, John Tomay Memorial Library, Georgetown (Clear Creek County).

Vernon ("Skip") Betts, Rocky Mountain National Park, Estes Park.

Walt Borneman, Evergreen.

Danyel Brenner, Old Town Museum, Burlington (Kit Carson County).

Lenore Bright, Archuleta County Public Library, Pagosa Springs.

Sally Buckland, Empire (Clear Creek County).

William G. Buckles, Dept. of Archaeology, University of Southern Colorado, Pueblo (Pueblo County).

Wallace L. Chafe, Dept. of Linguistics, University of California, Santa Barbara (Caddoan languages).

Jean Charney, Fort Collins.

Ruth Marie Colville, Del Norte (Rio Grande County).

Marilyn Cox, Montrose County Historical Society, Montrose.

Dan Davidson, Museum of Northwest Colorado, Craig (Moffat County).

Carole A. Deterding, Durango Public Library, Durango (La Plata County).

Norma Edlund, Director, Salida Regional Library.

James E. Fell, Jr., Louisville.

Cara D. Fisher, Local History Center, Canon City Public Library (Fremont County).

Irene Francis, West Custer County Library, Westcliffe.

Zethyl Gates, Loveland (Larimer County).

John Gresham, North Park Pioneer Museum, Walden (Jackson County).

Bertha Grove, Language and Culture Committee, Southern Ute Indian Tribe, Ignacio.

Barbara Hanzas, Woodruff Memorial Library, La Junta (Otero County).

Sharon Johnson, Kiowa County Public Library, Eads.

Thomas Johnson, Cortez (Montezuma County).

Marne Keith Jurgemeyer, Fort Morgan Museum (Morgan County).

John Koontz, Dept. of Linguistics, University of Colorado, Boulder (Siouan languages).

Robert MacDaniel, Animas Museum, Durango (La Plata County).

Nancy Manly, Lake County Public Library, Leadville.

Leo McCoy, Wray (Yuma County).

Amy McCray, Huerfano County Public Library, Walsenburg.

Wick R. Miller, Dept. of Anthropology, University of Utah, Salt Lake City (Uto-Aztecan languages).

Alden Naranjo, Language and Culture Committee, Southern Ute Indian Tribe, Ignacio.

Dorothy Naranjo, Language Coordinator, Southern Ute Indian Tribe, Ignacio.

Allen Nossaman, San Juan County Historical Society, Silverton.

Charles Page, Gunnison (Gunnison County).

Douglas Parks, Dept. of Anthropology, Indiana University, Bloomington, IN (Caddoan languages, Kiowa Apache language).

Robert Rankin, Dept. of Linguistics, University of Kansas, Lawrence, KS (Siouan languages).

Imogene Rich, Gilpin Historical Museum, Central City (Gilpin County).

Janet Riley, Frontier Museum, Glenwood Springs (Garfield County).

Evelyn Rios, Public Library, Trinidad.

David Rood, Dept. of Linguistics, University of Colorado, Boulder (Siouan and Caddoan languages).

Zdenek Salzmann, Dept. of Anthropology, Northern Arizona University, Flagstaff (Arapaho language).

Virginia McConnell Simmons, Monte Vista (San Luis Valley).

June Simonton, Colorado Ski Museum, Vail (Eagle County).

Esther J. Stephens, Delta County Historical Society, Delta.

Allan Taylor, Dept. of Linguistics, University of Colorado, Boulder (Arapaho language).

Susan Touchstone, Las Animas Library (Bent County).

Sharron G. Uhler, Colorado Springs Pioneers Museum (El Paso County).

Lucille Wailes, Bennett (Adams County).

Lee Whiteley, Littleton (Elbert County).

Trina Zagar, the *Meeker Herald*, Meeker (Rio Blanco County).

REFERENCES

Allen, Mary Moore. *Origin of Names of Army and Air Corps Posts, Camps, and Stations in World War II in Colorado*. Goldsboro, NC: [the author, 1952]. Typescript in Denver Public Library.

Arps, Louisa Ward, & Elinor Eppich Kingery. *High Country Names: Rocky Mountain National Park*. Rev. ed. Estes Park: Rocky Mountain Nature Association, 1972.

Baskette, Floyd K. *Pronunciation Guide, Colorado*. [Boulder: Pruett Press, 1955].

Cobos, Rubén. *A Dictionary of New Mexico and Southern Colorado Spanish*. Santa Fe: Museum of New Mexico Press, 1983.

Colorado Writers' Project. Place Names of Colorado. [Denver: Public Library, 1954]. Originally compiled by the Colorado Writers' Project; published as a series "Place Names in Colorado" in *Colorado*, 1940 to 1943. Typescript in Denver Public Library.

Dawson, John Frank. *Place Names in Colorado: Why 700 Communities Were So Named, 150 of Spanish or Indian Origin*. [Denver: J. F. Dawson, 1954].

Ellis, Erl H. *That Word "Idaho."* Denver: University of Denver Press, 1951.

Farquhar, Francis Peloubet. Naming America's Mountains, the Colorado Rockies. [New York, 1961]. Article reprinted from the *American Alpine Journal*, 1961.

Hagen, Mary, (ed.). *Larimer County Place Names: A History of Names on County Maps*. (Fort Collins Corral of Westerners, publication no. 2.) Fort Collins: Old Army Press, 1984.

Koehler, Olga Hazel. Place Names in Colorado: A Comparative Study. M.A. thesis, University of Denver, 1927. Copy in Denver Public Library.

Matthews, Ruth Estelle. A Study of Colorado Place Names. M.A. thesis, Stanford University, 1940. Copy in Denver Public Library.

Omni Gazetteer of the United States of America. Vol. 8, *Mountain States*. Detroit: Omnigraphics, 1991.

Page, Charles Albert. *What's in a Name? In the Gunnison Country*. Gunnison: Page Books, [1974].

Pearl, Richard M. *Nature's Names for Colorado Communities.* Colorado Springs: Earth Science Publishing Co., 1975.

Richie, Eleanor L. Spanish Place Names in Colorado. *American Speech* 10(2):87-92 (1935).

Simmons, Virginia McConnell. Hispanic Place Names of the San Luis Valley. (*San Luis Valley Historian*, 23:3.) Alamosa: San Luis Valley Historical Society, 1991.

Stewart, George R. *American Place Names.* New York: Oxford University Press, 1970.

Trager, George L. Some Special Place Names of Colorado. *American Speech* 5(3):203-207 (1935).

U.S. Dept. of Commerce. Bureau of the Census. 1990 Census of Population and Housing. *Summary Population and Housing Characteristics (1990 CPH-1-7): Colorado.* Washington: GPO, 1991.

Walther, Lou. *Old Names and Golden Splendors.* Boulder, 1983. (Mostly on Boulder County.)